A Little Boy in Paradise, Seco, KY

*To Tim -
Thanks
Obie W Spicer
Thanks for
Everything*

Obie W. Spicer, Jr.

BEARHEAD PUBLISHING

- BhP -

Brandenburg, Kentucky

BEARHEADPUBLISHING
- BhP -
Brandenburg, Kentucky
www.bearheadpublishing.com

A Little Boy in Paradise, Seco, KY
by Obie W. Spicer, Jr.

Cover Design by Bearhead Publishing
Cover Concept by Obie W. Spicer, Jr.
Thanks to Jim Clark, Obie's neighbor, for the back cover photograph.

First Printing - July 2015

ISBN: 978-1-937508-39-5
1 2 3 4 5 6 7 8 9

Proudly printed in the United States of America.

A Little Boy in Paradise, Seco, KY

Dedication

To all the people that have encouraged me to write this life-time so far. Especially to my Mom for my birth. I was born in Seco, KY at the age of 9 months old.

My mom! Believe me, she is always the beginning of this. Nearly 100 years old. She says I was the most beautiful baby born and that she really wanted another baby. I am her favorite. I bet my dad might have though that at the time.

If there has ever been an angel born on earth, it must have been my mother. The most loving, giving, caring person I have ever known.

Thanks, Mom.

Thanks to my wife, Linda. She has read this book at least 5 times. Correcting my mistakes, from spelling to have written the same thing twice, and for all her support during this venture. Thank you my sweetheart of 53 wonderful years.

Thanks to my daughters, Deborah and Rebecca, for their support, and their help with the computers.

Chapter One
The Utter Story

I will start with an encounter at the Seco Company store. I was probably 6-7 years old. I knew what utters were, but not by that name. We called them tits.

Us boys went to the store to get some Vienna sausage, weiners, crackers and a pop. What a life we had. Whatever we wanted, charge it to my dad. If only I had known how hard he worked for me. I miss him so much.

Obie and friends in his back yard
1 Ben Osborne 2 Daniel Hall 3 Obie Jr. 4 Peanut Hall
5 Roger Rudd 6 Daryele Hall 7 Clydie Quillen

Getting back to the tits. Lettie Struckland was her name. A wonderful person, wife, mother, Christian. She was at the cash register counter to pay for her groceries. Us boys were behind her in line to pay for our stuff, me, Clydie, Ben, Tony, Roger, Peanut, Ernest and Gene. There were more. We were going to the woods. We were a rough bunch—we thought.

Lettie wore a sack dress to take care of her big, short body. Even we knew this. Probably had 7-10 kids. Who knows. When miners came out on strike, they had kids. Time off from work, play time.

Getting back to Lettie. She had a baby with her, maybe less than a year old, maybe older. When you're my age, who cares. Anyway, this baby started screaming to the top, as loud as it could. I thought somebody was killing it. No! It was hungry. How was I to know. Mrs. Proffit was the cashier, beautiful woman. As I said, we were a bunch of tough guys. Get prepared.

Lettie laid this baby on the check-out counter, pulled her left or right arm out of her dress. Here came this big tit. I mean big. Didn't know at the time what was happening. This baby went quiet. As I said, she laid the baby on its back on the check-out counter. She put this big tit in its mouth. Milk ran down both sides of its mouth. We though the baby was going to drown or die of not breathing. Didn't take long, must have drank a quart or more. Lettie pulled her arm back in her dress, charged her groceries, took her baby, and walked out. As I said earlier, we charge our stuff. The coal company would deduct this at the end of the week form the miners paycheck.

The bunch of us charged out with Vienna sausage, crackers and pop. Probably had a Grapette or R.C. Cola. Then we took to the woods. Ready to conquer the world. For a day - until tomorrow. Once, we got a thousand miles away, which was really about a mile from our houses. But we were alone in our secluded place. We would eat our feast, talk about the Indians watching us behind the big trees. Sometimes we would dress like Indians, faces and all. Some kind of purple weed - it was hard to get off.

We stayed in the woods till evening. Our parents never worried about us like today. Nothing or nobody was going to hurt us or kidnap us. Never had a worry.

Most of our dads worked days - day shift they called it. Our dads would go to the bath house where the miners bathe before going home. They were black from coal dust. The only thing white were their eyes and teeth.

I would be waiting on my dad to get off his shift. He would see me and—that big smile and those white teeth. He would sorta hug me and take my hand. I would go with him to take a shower. We would go home. I was with my hero. I sure do miss him! We walked home, don't remember what we talked about. Probably not much. I probably told him my day's adventures, saw Indians, killed 5 rattlesnakes, ran 2 bears away. He believed every word. We would get home, mother would have supper nearly ready. We usually had pork chops, chicken or beef liver, beans, potatoes and cornbread. Everyday, I mean every day. Drinks would be milk, tea, water. By supper time, I was one hungry dude. We might have chocolate pie or some kind of cake. My favorite cake, just plain white cake. Still is—never was much on sweets.

The rest of the evening was spent with Mom and Dad. Maybe later Dad would take me to get an ice cream cone— vanilla—my favorite. More about this later in another chapter. We would come home and get ready for bed. I would go to sleep watching the coal train go by my bedroom window. The sound of the rail wheels would put me to sleep—clickedy clack—clickedy clack. Goodnight. I was getting ready for another day. Tomorrow, maybe capture some Indians.

Chapter Two
My First Bike

It was in the early summer, getting a little warm. All us boys were getting things ready for summer and things to do. Not many of us had bicycles, really didn't need one, never though about it. We did pretty good on our feet, didn't go very far from home. Actually we stayed in our little town of Seco, KY. To us boys, it was the whole world. Didn't have T.V. so how did we know. Our own little paradise.

Getting back to the charge to my dad thing, you could go to the company store and order things also. They had catalogs you could look through, order and get it within a few weeks.

My brother, Johnny, and Paul Patrick apparently wanted bikes, unbeknown to their dads or anyone else in the world. The L&N Railroad Company had a passenger train and Seco had a depot. They would stop and drop off things that people ordered from all over the country. There were men that worked for the South East Coal Company that actually ordered wives from different cities. They would arrive on the trains. The man would be waiting for her on the day she was to be there. All he ever saw were pictures of her. I never actually saw one, but I guess having one is better than not having one at all. She never saw him either, only a picture. Back to the bikes. Must have been pretty ugly women. One day the train stopped, dropped off the stuff people had ordered. In all this stuff were two big boxes. I actually saw them. They were probably 6 ft. long, 1 ft. wide, 4 ft. tall. They carried all this stuff in the store. They would take it upstairs to the storage area. Me and Roger Rudd, Ben Osborne and maybe more of the bunch saw the big boxes. What could these be?

Apparently, whoever was in charge of notifying people that had ordered this stuff, notified them. One of them was my dad. I miss him so much. He had no idea what he had ordered. He hadn't. I guess he went to see the mystery order.

Obie Lee Spicer, Sr.

Here was this big box with my brother's name on it. I guess. John Spicer, South East Coal Company, ordered by Obie Spicer, employed by South East Coal Company. I can remember my dad bringing this big box home. He began to cut it open. When he got all the edges cut, he said, "It looks like a bike." My brother, Johnny, was standing there. Dad looked at it and said, "I didn't order this." Johnny said he and Paul Patrick ordered one each. These things were beautiful, a Schwinn bicycle—top of the line bikes at the time. Dad didn't say a word, put the bike together. It was black and white, white wall tire, shocks up front and back, headlight. Beautiful, horn and all. It probably cost more than my daddy made in a week. He didn't say a word. I miss him.

JOHNNY SPICER SR.
SECO SCHOOL PICTURE

I was probably in school, first or second grade—which I hated. I asked Dad if I could have a bike. I didn't want one like Johnny had—too much stuff, I guess. I wasn't very big but thought I was. He would never say no to me; my mom would.

Finally, not long after Johnny got his bike, Dad took me to Neon, KY to the Western Auto Store. I walked in not knowing why. The next thing my daddy said was "Pick you out a bicycle." I didn't know, I looked and looked. When you are 5-6 years old, you don't look at prices. I guess you look at colors and sizes to fit you. Here it was—red and white. Western Flyer. Simple. No shocks, no horn, no light. This was it. Best I can remember, it was $29.00 (A little white tag hanging down from the handle bar). Dad asked me which one I wanted. I told him. He said, "Okay." He asked me if I wanted anything else. What a question!! I picked out those things you stick in your handle bar grips. Hang down, red and white. Cool tassels. I got a siren, put on the fork of your bike. This little wheel rubbed on the tire. You pulled a chain connected to the handlebar. When you did this, it sounded just like a siren. Really did. This got me in trouble more than once.

Tom Greer was the town policeman. He was a big man, dressed in a uniform and wore two big pistols. Must have been 45 caliber. He said I was disturbing people with the siren. Believe me it sounded exactly like one, so I did quiet down a little. He liked me a lot. I would walk with him in the evenings; sometimes to check and make sure things were okay in Seco, KY before dark. I think he made me his deputy. I got along with everybody. I always liked older people. Get to that later. As I said, my daddy would do most anything for me. I miss him.

I got the bike, tassels, siren and all. We took the bike home. Daddy put the tassels on the bike. I might have been 5 or 6—didn't know how to ride a bike. Actually, it was a little bit too big. My toes barely touched the pedals. My brother, Johnny—5 years older (he was probably 11—me 5-6) when I got this bike. Most of us guys my age started getting bikes after I got one. We must have ridden these machines a million miles—say the next two or three years. Maybe more.

These were some of the best times. I still think about my Western Flyer bike. Siren, tassels and all. I still have a bike made out of titanium. Maybe weighs a few pounds. Maybe five. Gears galore. Nothing like the big boy red Western Flyer. The one I have now is a Cannondale. Seat hurts. Never will get used to it.

Us boys made jumps. They call them ramps now. One day, we were jumping and I thought I was the best. Jumped pretty high, came down and cut my chin. Four stitches later Dr. Wright took care of that. He was really good at this kind of stuff. He drank a lot, so they said.

We would ride our bikes to Pine Mountain maybe 5 miles away. Look it up. Big mountain. We would try to ride down not using our brakes. I don't think any of us did this. If you ever got a chance, you should try to go. It is beautiful, my home.

Chapter Three
My First Horse

Most boys would say my first pony. I know it sounds a little bit far fetched, but this is the way it actually happened. I might be 9 years old, you know how that is. Doesn't matter much.

Mr. Ray Wilder worked at South East Coal Company with my dad. They would come and sit around talking during the day on the store porch. Can't remember exactly.

Mr. Wilder asked me if I would like a horse. I was ready. He wanted to trade his horse for my bike. He said his son wanted a bike and he didn't need the horse. Sounded good to me. I could ride a horse, not pedal a bike. Smart or what. I was probably more of a cowboy than a bike rider anyway. I had my bedroom full of cowboy stuff. I had wallpaper of nothing but desert—mule train, wagons, Indians, Roy Rogers pictures, Gene Autry, Whip Wilson, Hopalong Cassidy and Lone Ranger.

My mom got bed cover somewhere probably from Alden's catalog. They were covered wagons—sheets and all. I had a cool bedroom. I had a great mommy. I was her last and favorite child.

Getting back to the horse trading. I told my brother, Johnny, Mr. Wilder would trade me this horse for my bike. He wanted it for his boy. Didn't know him, they lived in Milestone, KY. Seemed a million miles away. Didn't know where this place was. Johnny is 5 years older than me. I was probably 8 or 9 years old. I begged him to help me get my bike to Mr. Wilder's home. He finally agreed to this adventure.

It was a long way to go by highway, not too far over the mountain trail. He pushed this bike maybe 2 miles across this mountain trail. He knew where he was going. We got to their house. Mr. Wilder and family were waiting for us. There stood this big black horse. I mean Big! His legs were taller than me. This family had a lot of people in it, probably 8 or 9—plus chickens and dogs. Sure wasn't Seco, KY. Pretty long holler the way it looked to me. Way back in the mountains. This was my beginning of horse trading. Anyway, we traded. Didn't have a saddle, only a rope bridle. They helped me get on this big monster. Here he went. Maybe we would get to Seco, KY. Thanks to my big brother, we finally made it. Here I was going home with my first horse.

Obie W. Spicer, Jr.

It was in the early evening. My daddy was sitting on the back porch. He had just gotten off from work. Here I came down the alley on this big black horse. I rode up the yard where he was. He looked up with that big smile. "Where did you get that big horse? Who does it belong to?" I didn't know what to say. I think he helped me off. I told him I traded my bike for it. He said how did this happen. I told him about Mr. Wilder and all. As I said, my daddy would let me do most anything. I miss him. He asked where was I going to keep this horse. Guess what! I didn't think about that.

South East Coal Company had lots of land. Mr. Ted Dingus kept his horse on some of it. I told Daddy about this. Was I thinking or what? Daddy went that evening to Ted's house and told him the situation. Of course, Mr. Dingus told Daddy to take my horse and let him loose there.

I didn't know if the horse was a male or female. Didn't matter. Mr. Wilder said the horse was called Nellie. Sounded good to me. I kept his horse for awhile on the property. Too big for me to ride much.

A Little Boy in Paradise, Seco, KY

Obie W. Spicer, Jr.

Can't remember who it was, somehow I traded Nellie for a pony. What a trade. I could get on this pony with one jump. I named him Spot. He was black and white. Didn't have much—a bridle, no saddle. I thought I was Little Beaver. You know, Red Rider and Little Beaver or the Lone Ranger and Tonto. I loved Spot. We were the best buddies ever.

Obie W. Spicer, Jr.

It was getting cooler weather; fall of the year. I guess when you are a young boy you don't think much about these things. Living one day at a time. Fun is all that matters. Know what I mean.

They called it Thanksgiving or something with all this stuff. Didn't like much of the stuff. Dressing was my favorite part. Mom fixed good dressing and mashed potatoes. The one thing I did know was Christmas. I never did care much about cold weather. Still don't. We would go sleigh riding and burn car tires to stay warm.

You would get the black stuff from the smoke up your nose. It smelled awful. The snow was pretty and the snow cream tasted like vanilla ice cream—milk, snow, sugar and maybe a little bit of vanilla flavoring.

Getting back to the big Christmas thing. The little Methodist church in Seco would have Christmas plays. I guess this was the thing to do. We would dress up like a bunch of freaks—camels, sheep, angels. We all tried to remember what to say. Who cared. I guess this made the preacher and parents happy. I loved this church. We would go every Sunday. My sister, Tressie Lynn Spicer, would play too. All of us kids would march down the aisle. Mrs. Tuggle, the preacher's wife, I think would play Onward Christian Solders. It felt good. We all stepped together probably the only time any of us were really serious. We all knew God was watching us. If we didn't, we would all go straight to Hell. I've probably heard more about Hell than anything else in church. Sure don't want to go there.

Getting back to Christmas. Everybody would come home for Christmas from all over, Ohio, Tennessee, Georgia and wherever else. Aunt Ruby—mom's sister, my favorite aunt of all, still is. She is 90 years old at this writing. She always got me something special at Christmas anyway. Christmas morning, I opened my package from Aunt Ruby. It was a gift I will never forget. A Lone Ranger kit: two pistols, holsters, eye mask, wrist cuffs, chaps, bullets and all.

If you don't know what cap pistols are—the caps were rolls of red paper with a little bit of gun powder on it. You put the rolls on a little stem; when you pulled the trigger, it would move the roll; the hammer would hit the cap. Sounded like a bullet being fired. Pretty cool. Those days are gone. All computers and videos. Too bad for the kids. What a life to be a little boy in Seco, KY.

Chapter Four
Grade School in Seco, KY

The school was a big area. Not far from where I lived. The ball field was there too. It probably didn't take a few minutes to walk to the school.

I didn't know what school would be like; they didn't have kindergarten then. I really didn't know what to expect.

My mother told me I had to go to school. I was 6 years old. My mommy took me to school the first day. I think she knew I probably wouldn't like it; she was right. I didn't like not being able to do what I wanted. She left me at this place in a big room early in the morning. I didn't stay long. I left this place and came home. Mommy was there and wanted to know what was wrong. I really didn't know. She took me back to school. I stayed. You did what your mother said or you would regret it. Know what I mean?

Listen to me folks; you could not have a knife in your possession. This was part of your body. If the teacher did find one, they would take it and put it in their desk drawer. Knife gone until end of school year.

I know the best part of school was recess. We would play Mumble Peg. A knife. Don't have time to explain all of this but this I will tell you; we had a pond behind the school. This pond would produce tad-poles, which make frogs. Still don't understand all of this. One day maybe a few (maybe second grade) of us boys decided to put these little frogs in the teacher's desk drawers. We must have put 10-20 in there. Don't remember her name. I really didn't care, but the morning she opened the desk drawer, we were in class. We though she was going to die. Screaming! The little frogs were jumping out on her. I was scared she was going to die. Mr. Whitaker was the principal of grade school. He had to be the uglist man in the whole world. Mean, short. I didn't like him the first time I saw him. Probably under-educated. Thought he was very very smart. Stupid in my assumption. School was very strict. Couldn't do much; sit and wait for recess. We would play in the ballpark. Shoot marbles or mumble peg.

The gang, you know by now who this is: me, Tony, Clyde, Ben, Peanut, Daniel, we figured out how to kill Mr. Whitaker. I would shoot him, bury him under the schoolhouse and they would never find him. Of course, we didn't have a gun. Mr. Whitaker had lived. Don't know what happened to him; really don't give a damn.

Betty Terry was her name. Sad but very true. We didn't know what was wrong with her, but she would fall over in the classroom. Tongue out, shaking like a fish. We would look. They would finally get her up. She was having an epileptic fit. That's what they called it. They said she died drowning in a creek at her grandparents house.

These are my days of Seco, KY grade school. Don't know what happened, but she was a pretty black haired girl from Seco, KY. She would kiss you maybe. She would shake and roll on the floor. They would pull her tongue out, probably would die. I miss you Betty. Memories are all we have left.

Chapter Five
County Doctors

Dr. Collins and Mrs. Collins was the county doctor and his wife, hired by the county to take care of the people. The County Health Department. They were both ugly. I mean ugly. Once a year, they would come to our school to make sure we were healthy. They would give us shots. I think the shots were worse than the illness. They would make us get in a line. Mr. Whitaker, the principal, I told you this, I guess he thought he was God (acted like it). I said we couldn't find a gun to kill him.

We would line up. Mr and Mrs. Collins were there. First, let me tell you this. They would drive a black car; they dressed in black. We all were scared of them. We all thought they were from Hell. The line was long. All of us would line up.

We would walk from the first floor to the second floor—there stood the doctors from Hell. They had a table with trays of things to give shots with and teeth pullers—pliers. The needles were long. They would give several shots from the same syringe. Needle long, hurt like the dickens. Mrs. Collins would give the shots. The needle was very long. Lots of the kids would cry. The doctors didn't care. They never had kids. Probably never had any sexual activity. Pretty bland looking. When you got past your shots, they would check out your teeth. Open mouth. If Dr. Collins thought you had a bad tooth, he would pull, no numbing or nothing. He would take his pliers. She would open your mouth. He would pull your teeth. No questions asked. The kids would scream. Didn't have any kind of medicine to kill the hurt of pulling a tooth. You know when they pulled a tooth. Screaming from kids, who had a tooth pulled. We all knew they enjoyed this. This was a terrible experience for children to go through. But this is what you did in Seco, KY.

Chapter Six
The Barber Shop

The barber shop was the place to meet. If you wanted to know anything, go to the barber shop.

Clarence Boyd was the barber. He was a nice man. He charged ten cents for a hair cut.

Mr. Boyd had one leg—the other was artificial. Don't know how he lost it. Probably in the war or his wife might have cut it off.

As I said earlier, I didn't forget anything. Mother took me to get a hair cut. I didn't like it at all.

Mr. Boyd collected Roosevelt dimes. He got many for a hair cut. The shop wasn't very big, maybe 20 X 20 feet. Had a few waiting chairs, big ceiling fan, no air conditioning, couple of windows. There was someone always in the shop. I was there a lot. The barber shop was heated by steam heat. A big radiator was against the wall. South East Coal Company heated the company store, hospital, Fountain restaurant, post office and theater with steam heat from coal. They had their own hot water system. They also heated the bathhouse where the miners would bathe after their day's work.

One day I was in the shop probably talking to Mr. Boyd. He was a very nice man. Woodie Fitch came in the shop, got a hair cut. We were talking, I liked to talk to older men. Learned a lot I think.

Woodie got a broom, swept the floor for Mr. Boyd. When he was finished, I took the broom by one end and Woodie took the other. We begin to swing around. I guess I turned loose. When I did, I hit the radiator. It must have put 5 or 6 big cuts on my head. Blood was everywhere. They took me to the hospital across the street. Mom worked in the Fountain which was down under the hospital. They got her to come upstairs. I was lying on the table in Dr. Wright's operating room. Mom came in. She saw all the blood on my head, and she fainted dead as could be. I was in better shape than she was. They took care of her first, then the doctor stitched my wounds. I was fine. Went back to the usual stuff. What a great life in Seco, KY.

There was a big oak tree outside next to the barber shop. The men would sit out there and whittle. Of course, I would sit with them. As I said, I liked older people. I learned to whittle as good as they did. Had to have a real sharp knife. I had a few. Cedar wood was the best, smelled so good. The joy of whittling was to see who could get the longest curl. You had to take your easy time, real fine cutting. Sometimes you could get them several inches long.

All the men chewed tobacco. Usually Brown Mule, Star, Mammoth Cave Twist, Beechnut or Apple. The first time I chewed, I got sick—I mean sick, puked, dizzy. But you kept doing this until you got it right. I could chew and spit and whittle as good as any of the men. We would whittle piles of shavings. Cedar smelled so good. The men would give me tobacco to chew. I couldn't buy any.

Sid Vance chewed a lot. He could take a whole plug of tobacco and put it in his mouth at one time. His jaw would stick out. Don't know how he did it. He got real bad sick, cut his tongue out, jaw bone. Never did look the same. They said the tobacco did it. He didn't live a long time. Probably cancer. Don't think they knew what it was.

I guess Mr. Boyd lived a long time. But he died. Still had the barber shop in Seco, KY. After he died, I don't think they had another barber shop there. The gang went in the shop after he died to see if anything was in it of interest. Guess what we found in the back room of the barber shop? It was his artificial leg!! Man was it Big. It was his whole leg. They must have cut his leg off at his hip, a little below. The knee joint would bend. It still had a sock and shoe on it. We would put our short legs down in it. We had a long leg and a short one. We played a while with it. Left the barber shop. Don't remember much after that. Mr. Boyd was a nice man. I liked him a lot. Wondered what happened to all those Roosevelt dimes.

This was the best barber shop ever. I can still smell the powder and tonic. This is Seco, KY. What a place to live. Maybe this is why I am now a barber.

Chapter Seven
The Humane Society

I know what you are thinking; there was nothing like this way back then. Well, there was! The gang had one.

When the cats had kittens, there were many cats in Seco, KY, they had kittens—many. We would get the kittens, their eyes weren't even open. We probably got at least a hundred or more. We would put them in a big bag and throw them over the bridge in Seco. Don't know what happened to them. They would go down the creek to somewhere else. We did the pups, you know from dogs, the same way. If we didn't do this, there would have been a million cats and dogs. We did the same with rats. Some times we would take two rats and tie their legs together with rope, hang them over a clothesline. They would fight for a long time. We would leave them. Got boring. We had other plans. There was never an overflow of cats or dogs. The gang took care of that. In spite of all of this, there were still many dogs and cats. Everybody had dogs and cats. They would have many.

Mr. Green was his name. He liked his liquor. One Saturday, he was drinking a lot as many of the men did. Us boys were watching him. We were in #1 holler (they had names for areas in Seco).

The dogs were following Mr. Green, barking at him. As I said, he was drinking, probably drunk. He had a pistol in his pocket. Guess he got mad. He pulled this pistol out, shot and killed this dog. Blood ran on the road. He would get another dog to come to him. By the time he got through killing the dogs, he had a big pile of dogs. Blood was running down the road. He probably killed at least 30 dogs. All piled up. We left Mr. Green with this problem. Don't know what happened after that. We had more things to get to.

Mr. Green was a fine person, had a family and all. Probably went to church and all that stuff. He worked hard, played hard. He and my daddy worked together. If I were guessing where he went, Heaven or Hell—Heaven would be my guess. Judge not. God is what matters.

Well, so much for the Humane Society. We didn't get paid for the job but we sure did help in the numbers. Plus, we had a good time doing it. What a life. This is what and how it was in Seco, KY.

Most men in Seco carried pistols, this was and still is a tradition in the mountains of Eastern Kentucky. I have one with me most of the time. Always in my vehicle. Also have a permit to do this.

Chapter Eight
Town Drunks

How does one start this chapter. There were very many, some not as bad as others. These men worked hard for the coal company, but they liked their liquor.

The Sam, they called him. That's all I knew him by. His dad called him that. I remember he would sit on the railroad tracks, close to the Methodist Church. I know that he was a Christian; I know he went to Heaven. I will see him some day there. Judge not.

The Sam would get all the dogs barking. He was a good man. He got killed in a truck crossing the tracks at Seco. He was a delivery man for the company. I will get back to this later in another chapter.

Mr. Green, as I have written about earlier, was one of these men. Very fine citizen and parent. Worked hard but had a good time. I don't remember seeing their wives. Don't know what they did—cooked and took care of the kids.

These men would work all week but on the weekends, they would drink liquor or moonshine. I know now that's what they called it.

Mr. Champion was one of these men. He was a wonderful man. I loved him very much. He liked his liquor. Us boys would follow him around Seco. He would go behind the grade school. He would stagger and fall down. Take his bottle form his pocket, drink all that was left, throw the bottle and fall on his knees. He would try to talk. Probably needed to pee. Take it out, you know. Pee a lot. He would then fall over, go to sleep I guess. We would leave him alone. I know he went to be with the Lord when he died. I don't know when. I will see him in Heaven if there is a Heaven.

Lonnie Fleener had to be the world's greatest piano player. He had a piano in his house. This was in #2 Holler. That's what they called. it. The piano cost more than the house. Jerry Lee Lewis couldn't begin to play like him. We would go to listen to him. He would play on Sunday evenings, probably after church. People from town would come. Mostly men. He had a little glass sitting on his piano. They or someone would pour him a drink in the glass. He would start playing a little on his piano. They would fill his glass. The more he drank the better he would play. All the Christians would go to church on Sunday to pray but they would go on Sunday evening to hear Lon Fleener play. The more the liquor he had, the more he played. The more he played, the more we should pray. We will see him in Heaven some day. I know he will be in Heaven. I miss you Lon Fleener.

Mr. Green was part of this. The man that killed all the dogs.

Chapter Nine
My Best Neighbor

Mr. Fitch was our neighbor. He wasn't a real town drunk as none of these men really were, but they liked their booze. He was a veteran and all that stuff. He was really good to me. Take me with him to Neon on Saturday and buy me candy and pop. We would go to the movie in Neon on Saturday. There was a movie about the war. The Japs—that's what they called them. I think Mr. Fitch was probably in the war. The Japanese soldiers would take the American soldiers in this room. You could hear them screaming. They would bring the soldiers out, drag them down the halls. They would be screaming; no fingers, no ears, no tongues. It was a horrible movie. Mr. Fitch was crying when we left.

We left, turned left and walked up the street. He said he was going to get a quart of milk. Sounded good to me. We got to Tuckers Restaurant. Thought we were going there. No, I was wrong. A couple of stores up was the Hub. It wasn't a grocery. A lot of men were in there. Mr. Fitch and I stood at the counter. He asked for a quart of milk. It was in a brown bag. I got a Grapette drink. He had a glass of something. Didn't know then it was whiskey. Plus, the bag—a bottle. Mr. Bentley owned the Hub. He was a bootlegger. Right in the middle of Neon, KY. We got in his car.

Went back to Seco. Mr. Fitch drove a Studebaker car. It was a pretty green car; I guess he drank his milk that evening.

What a day. Mr. Fitch was a nice man. He was a good friend of mine. I still think of him. I know he went to Heaven. Another day in Seco, KY. What a place to live.

Taking a few minutes to get a sip of my cherry pie and pipe.

Chapter Ten

The Hospital of Seco— Dr. Wright

This was the place to be for the gang. If the sirens went off in Seco, it meant something was wrong. Usually a miner was killed or seriously injured. Mr. Reach was one of the men. A big piece of rock fell on him. He was crushed. They took him away to Lexington, KY. He was gone a long time it seemed. When he came home, he didn't look like himself. His face was different, looked like a different person. I guess Dr. Wright tried his best at the hospital in Seco.

Many men were killed in the mine. My best buddy was Peanut Hall. They lived behind us. One day the sirens went off. It wasn't good. His daddy got killed.

One day we were swimming in the creek. His daddy was also a preacher. Our parents didn't want us to swim in the creek. We thought his dad was at work. Wrong. Mr. Hall came from behind. Peanut hit him. Peanut didn't know it was his daddy. Peanut said, "You son of a bitch." All you could see was Peanut flying about 3 feet off the ground. There was a big family there. When a miner got killed, the family couldn't live there for a long time. They moved to Fleming.

Dr. Wright was a good man. He drank a lot they said. He probably saved my life. I would get pneumonia I can remember. He would come to our house. He put his finger down my throat and pulled the phlegm out. He gave me the first Penicillin shot in Seco. I was in the hospital at this time.

When a miner got injured, they would bring him there first to the hospital. The gang—us boys—would go to the hospital to see what was happening.

One evening a miner was injured. They brought him to the hospital. The gang was waiting. They carried him into the operating room. Dr. Wright was waiting. They put him on the table. The room always smelled of alcohol and ether. The table had a pull-out slide on the side. Dr. Wright pulled his arm and put it on the slide out part. We would stand in the hallway and watch. We did this all the time. The nurse put the ether mask over his face. The smell was so strong that it nearly put you to sleep also. Dr. Wright looked at his damaged arm. I guess he decided the arm had to be removed. We stood there and watched. He actually took this saw—looked like a hack saw. Probably stainless steel. He laid it in a tray. Probably alcohol. He then picked it up and laid it on the miner's arm. We watched Dr. Wright saw his arm in to. Then Dr. Wright sewed the skin. He pulled the skin over the bone then sewed it all together. I can't remember the miner's name, but I will. I will put it in this space: Mr. Newson. I saw him some days later, no arm below his elbow. He still had a job at Seco South East Coal Company.

The dog was another day. Somebody brought this dog to the hospital. Had something in his eye. They put the dog on the operating table, gave him ether. I can still smell ether. What a terrible smell. The dog was asleep. Dr. Wright cut the eye out, laid it on a tray. He took a big needle and thread, sewed the eyelids together. Us boys left. Seco had a one-eyed dog. There was always something happening at the hospital. Us boys loved it.

One evening, the ambulance pulled in. Mr. Quillan was

lying on the bed. He had been shot in the head, on the side—temple area. They carried him upstairs to the hospital. He was lying in the hallway. It always smelled like the purple medicine they put on everything. Us boys stood and looked at Mr. Quillan. Blood was slowly running out of his wound. He would jerk a little, his whole body would shake. He stopped jerking. Probably died then. Don't know. We left. Mr. Quillen probably went to Heaven. He was a good man.

What a life in Seco, KY.

I think Peanut became a preacher later in life. The whipping probably helped from cussing. Peanut, I love you if you are still living.

Chapter Eleven
The Honey Wagon—
A Septic Tank on Wheels

What a wonderful time for the gang. We would follow the honey wagon around town. They had a big truck. These men would turn a toilet over making sure the hole was clear to get the stuff out. You know, poop and stuff. The stuff the men put in the toilets smelled good and clean. Some kind of powder, pink in color.

Us boys wanted to see what they scooped out of the toilets. Everything: socks, paper, orange peelings, lots of toilet paper, lots of rubbers or gold rings. This is what they called them. I don't know why the men used them. They had children anyway. all the strikes and such. I know now but didn't know then.

Her name was—maybe I should not reveal her name. A nice neighbor, wonderful person, Christian woman. Very proper and all that stuff. I guess she liked to make babies, or go to bed a lot. The gang was at their toilet when the honey wagon men turned the toilet over. We looked down into the hole. There was probably 100 or maybe 300 rubbers floating on the poop. They looked like eyeballs looking at you. This nice lady walked out the wooden walk, looked down and saw a lot of this in the toilet. She went into a crazy state of mind. She told us boys to get out of there. We didn't know then but we did later. We never mentioned this. It is still our secret or a memory of days in Seco, KY. She died a few years ago. I loved her so much. She gave me a lot of candy, cookies, food. I know she went to Heaven. I bet she is smiling at me right now and laughing. I did love to make love. I miss you Mrs. _____. I will see you again.

The gang didn't know what the men that had the honey wagon did with the toilet stuff or where they came from. We only saw them once a year. One day we followed them. They went maybe a mile or less to a cemetery. They drove the truck, backed it up. They put the poop and paper or what was in the toilets over the cemetery. I guess it made the grass grow, plus, the remains in the cemetery didn't care. Then they would put more pink powder on the ground. Smelled good, made the grass green. Who cared. They were all Baptist. Only Baptist goes to Heaven. Ha Ha.

This is the way it was in the town of Seco, KY. What a place to live. Never a worry. Play all day, go to bed, wake up ready for another day. I still love and remember these days. I can still smell the pink flavor.

Chapter Twelve
The Carnivals

What a life. No stress, no fear of anything to hurt you, no shootings or wars. Just fun and happiness. Not like today. If only the children could live like this.

The carnival would come every year—maybe. When they did, they would put the tents and stuff in the ballpark next to the grade school. Lots of lights, rides and stuff. We could get cotton candy, play games. Men would try to win dolls for their wives or girls. The main attraction was the women. It was called the Hootchie Cootchie women show. Us boys would stand out front. Couldn't go inside. These girls would come outside on stage, do their thing and go inside.

The man with the speaker would say: The girls would shake it up one side and roll it down the other.

We could not go in; we were too young. We would slide under the tent and watch the women. They would come on the stage one at a time. Naked of course. All of them were white—really white. All they had on were shoes. High heel shoes. Some had big breasts—some not big. They would dance or move a little. The men would whistle, holler—whatever. One of the girls took a cigarette—she put it in her female part. Actually made smoke come out. The men went crazy. One man—can't mention his name—went on the stage, took the cigarette and puffed on it. Then he tried to kiss and hug the girl. There was a fight between them. Got pretty rough. They closed the show down. I can still see the girls and the bodies.

My dad might have been there at some of the shows. My mom would have killed him if she had known.

This was the last carnival in Seco, KY. What a wonderful town this was, to be a part of history and I was part of it.

This is the way it was in Seco, KY. What a place to grow and live as a boy—and I mean boy.

Chapter Thirteen
Sissies of Seco, KY

The gang was a tough bunch of guys. There was a few of the boys or whatever that acted a little different. Didn't know what was wrong with them. Their mothers treated them like girls—not boys. The mothers fixed them a house on Boss Hill. It had been a chicken house.

The mothers made a house for the boys (or girls). They put in mirrors, hose to wear, lipstick. A house like theirs. The boys would dress like girls. Can't tell who they were—a different group. One day we went to the place their mothers had made for them. We went in the playhouse. Threw the panties, lipstick out—clothes for girls. Then we tore the house up. Broke the poles that held the chicken house up. This was the end of the boys that were girls in Seco, KY.

We didn't know anything about gays or queers, but some of the boys or girls did turn out to be gay or queer. They died at a very young age—my neighbors. One of them married a teacher. He was also a teacher. She was very pretty. Don't know why she married him. They were married a short time. Didn't know why.

The rumor was he bought a rubber—never used it. She left him. She sure was pretty. Don't know what happened to her but he later died. Years later, he died of some illness. Probably AIDS.

This was the way it was in the wonderful town of Seco, KY.

This is the way of the world today. Only it was smaller. Same place. Different times.

Thanks Seco for my daughters. I was not gay or queer—but I had a Hell of a great time. What a place to grow up in. I was happy, happy.

I cannot judge a person. Only God can.

Only one person has told me he was gay. I saw him grow up from a child. Cut his hair—still do. He went to college. He now teaches school. Done this for 20 years or more. A very dear friend. My family. His dad was a dear friend. He was born a boy but should have been a little girl. He had all the little girl features. He goes to church. Very active in church. Sings in the choir. The people in church know this.

How can one judge another. Only God can.

The boys in Seco, KY had no idea what they were, but all of us boys knew they were different. They all went to church in the little Methodist Church with me and the gang. Played together everyday. Went to school together. Love all of them. Most have died. I know God takes care of those who love Him and have been forgiven and saved. I hope this is how it works. If not, we are in big trouble. Amen and amen.

Chapter Fourteen
The Lumber Truck— Gas Tanks

This is one of my best times or worst day of all. The true facts of Seco, KY. As I said we were a bunch of boys, who had to make our own way to have a good time.

South East Coal Company had their own trucks to haul their material to work with. They parked them in a big lot next to the lumber yard. I don't know how we started doing this, but we would get on the big flat beds of the trucks, take the gas caps off the gas tanks, lie down and smell the gas fumes from the tanks. Only once did we do this.

When you sniffed this stuff, you would get so dizzy you could not stand up. It was crazy. Millard Land was one of my best buddies. When you were so dizzy from this, you would actually stand up and walk off the big truck bed. It was probably 4 feet to the ground. Didn't hurt. You would walk right off the truck bed onto the ground. Thought you were falling 100 feet. Millard probably sniffed too much. He walked across the road into Mrs. Davidson's yard. He fell over, started to shake and quiver with foam coming from his mouth. He stopped moving. Mrs. Davidson came outside.

She saw him and started screaming. She ran to the hospital and got Dr. Wright (probably half looped). He looked at Millard and then at us. Asked what we had been doing. We knew we were in big trouble. Dr. Wright told us if we ever did this again he would tell our parents. I guess he smelled the gas fumes from Millard. Millard was okay. We never did this again. Sure was fun at the time.

Every time I get gas in my car, I can still get a little buzz from the fumes. I don't dare smell too much. I'm driving now, don't want to get caught for sniffing. Too old I guess.

What a time to live, what a life in Seco, KY. I loved this little town.

Think I will have another sip of my cherry pie.

Chapter Fifteen
Mr. Dingus' Car

I guess I was the one who would try anything—still do. We were in Number One Holler. This is where they keep the machines to the mines, the motors as they called them, to pull the coal from the mines. Mr. Dingus had a couple of old cars—Ford or Chevy. 1920 or later. He had them in a shed. One day we were in the holler playing. Here they were—these beautiful cars. We looked them over, as you can imagine. The gang, what a bunch.

I jumped up in the seat behind the wheel. I was probably 9 years old—more or less. Felt good. They dared me to drive the car out of the barn or shed. They pulled me out, could barely see the road, but I was the driver of this car. I started down this big hill toward the town of Seco, probably 1/2 mile or so. I mean straight down—curves and all. I probably went a few hundred feet—moving fast—very fast. I realized I would not make it very far—killing me or maybe more people. There was a silt pond on my left where they put junk from the mines and such. I drove the beautiful car into the pond. It sank as I was looking at it. There was a little part of the windshield sticking out of the mud. Mr. Dingus never knew what was the reason or who did this.

This was a good time in my town of Seco, KY. They talked about this a long time. They got the car out and Mr. Dingus was happy.

Chapter Sixteen
Lumber Yard—Tongue

Seco had their own sawmill or lumber yard where they cut and trimmed their own lumber to fit their needs. They had a big building where they would cut their wood and throw the shavings in a big pile down a big pipe. The gang put a diving board out of the door on top of the door into the shavings. One day we were diving off the board. I decided I would jump or dive. I got on the diving board, took a look and bounced on the board. I fell on the shavings. Felt real good. I started to climb up the shavings. When I got to the top. The diving board was right above me. I guess I stuck my tongue out (maybe to spit shavings out of my mouth). When I did, the board hit the top of my head. The force from the diving board hit my head; I bit my tongue between my teeth. It was a bad day for me.

I cut my tongue nearly in to. Blood was running out of my mouth like water. Didn't know what to do. The gang ran down the road to the water spigot. I put my mouth over the spigot. It felt good. I went to the hospital and Dr. Wright looked at it. I quit bleeding some while later. My tongue swelled really big. I couldn't stop bleeding. I couldn't eat or swallow. I drank a lot of milk and milk shakes.

I got over this. This was a good time in Seco, Ky. My tongue healed and I can still talk very well. What a life in Seco, Ky. Thanks Omar Champion, Kimmer Calahoun, Tony Taylor and Ben Osborne.

I think Omar jumped on the board. I was under it—that's what did my tongue—Don't worry, Omar. I'm good. He is still living in the mountains. See him now and then. Love you Omar. I know you will go to heaven.

Chapter Seventeen
The Fountain

The Fountain was the most wonderful place in the world.

When you first walked in—you would smell the hamburgers, pepper, milk shakes, cigarettes—Camels—of course. The first thing you saw was a glass case with knives—Barlow, Remington, case. Old knives now but not then. There was a big counter with stools, tables with seats or chairs. They even had menus. The best thing was grilled cheese and French fries, chocolate milk shake.

My mom worked at the Fountain. She was the most beautiful of all the waitresses.

Dr. Wright ate there every day. He would eat a steak. Mom told me he liked his steak rare, very rare. She said the blood was running, very runny.

Politicians would come to Seco to get votes. Mom said Happy Chandler came to the Fountain with his group to campaign. They ate steak and all the fine food at the Foundation. Mom said they left a nickel tip. She gave it back to him. What a prick he must have been. I am sure to this day he was.

I can still smell the burger, chili, vegetable soup, Camel cigarette smoke. If only you could. Thanks to Oakie Wright, Melda Burchwell, Virginia Creech for the fine food. I will always be with you. I know all of you are in the hands of the Lord Jesus Christ because of the way you lived and served the Lord in our little church in Seco, KY.

Chapter Eighteen
The Theatre

What a beautiful movie theatre this was. No around sound, no big entrance. It was below the hospital, behind the Fountain. One big building, same building.

We saw the best movies: Whip Wilson, Hoppalong Cassidy, Roy Rogers and many more.

Believe it or not, we had a lot of the best country music singers who traveled the roads of Kentucky. Lester Flatt and Earl Scruggs came to Seco, KY to play and sing. Hank Williams and all.

Can't remember all the cartoons out. They were great. Wish my grandkids could see them, Cal and Savannah.

Chapter Nineteen
Pie Supper

The theatre was used for many functions; parties, dinners and the most wonderful one was the pie supper. The women and wives would fix pies or cakes. The women would put their pies or cakes on a big table. Nobody knew who made them. The town people would sit down in the theatre seats. It was quite a time.

I think Mr. Preston was the one who was the auctioneer. He picked up a pie or cake and the men would start bidding. Whoever bid the highest price would share it with the girl or woman who made it. The women had to eat with the person who won. Sometimes it wasn't what the wives wanted—to eat with another man or boy. There were not any fights. We sure had some good pies and cakes.

The women would put all the cakes and pies on a big table. Everybody would eat them.

I don't know what they did with the money—probably gave it to the Seco Methodist Church. What a better place to put the money—in God's hands to help people who did need it.

Preacher Tuggle was a true man of the Lord. I only wish the preachers were like him today. Not for money or a big church but for the Lord and saving people. Preacher Tuggle, thank you for my being able to remember. I will see you in Heaven someday.

What a time in Seco, KY—my little part of Heaven.

Most of the pies and cakes were in boxes, decorated with ribbons, bows, lots of colors. Very pretty but no names on them. Beautiful! What a time we had. Didn't have a lot of money, but sure had a lot of love.

Chapter Twenty
Railroads—Wrecks, People Killed, Animals

The L&N Railroad ran in Letcher County. Big steam engines. They were powered by coal. They would put out black smoke and cinders. Sounded real good.

There were a lot of accidents. Men would get drunk and sit or fall asleep on the tracks. The train would run over them. Can you imagine that? They would find parts miles away, legs in one place, arms in another.

There were these railroad tracks that came through Seco. One day the delivery men, who delivered goods to people, didn't see the train approaching them at the crossing. The train hit them. Mr. Hall and Dewey Spears were in the truck. Mr. Hall was killed. Dewey was hurt pretty bad. He was my friend. Lost part of his ear, but okay.

Lots of dogs were killed. I can remember one cow being hit by the train. Parts of the cow were everywhere.

Chapter Twenty-One
Coal Trains and People Would Hobo Trains

My dad told me to <u>never</u> hobo a train—or jump on one to go to another town.

This man lived in Seco. He had only one leg, cut off at his knee. He got it cut off trying to hobo a train. He jumped on the tracks and then on the train. He fell and the wheels from the coal car cut off his leg. Very lucky, don't you think? He would ride his bike very well. He used a crutch on one pedal and his own leg on the other. Looked pretty funny, but it worked. His name was Carl Robinson. That is what I think. I was very young then. A true story. What a time I had in the town of Seco, KY.

Chapter Twenty-Two
Trading Dogs, Boots and Script

I was always trading something—knives, tools, shows, boots. I had dogs all the time. If a dog came to town, he would go to my home. One day, I found a pretty pig.

Hound dog, we had became friends as all the dogs of Seco, KY. This hound dog was a Blue Tick Hound, so I was told. He followed me all the time. One day, a man came to the barber shop. He asked who the dog belonged to—the Blue Tick Hound. Mr. Dingus told him the dog belonged to me. I didn't own the dog, but I had him. Possession wise—I guess I did own him. He wanted to know if I would sell the dog. Didn't care. My dog. There were lots of dogs. He told me he would like to buy my dog.

I don't know where he came from or what his name was. He wanted the dog really bad. I don't really remember the price. I would guess two or three dollars. I had no idea where this dog came from or where it went. But I made a little bit of money. Did pretty good. Probably bought a baseball or a new glove with the money. I never did without stuff to play with.

What a wonderful place to live—Seco, KY. Never a worry, no stress. The dogs were part of my life. People say dogs know;

know the smell of people who like them. Very true. I know they liked me.

Maybe the Blue Tick Hound was a good coondog, maybe a champion. I sure do hope so. Thanks for my little town of Seco, KY.

Chapter Twenty-Three
Boots—Tires

I was always doing something. Trading a lot. Still do. I would roll tires around town. Felt good. One day I was rolling my tire. Tony wanted it. He had on a pair of rubber boots. I told him I would trade my big tire for his boots. He said okay. We traded. Good deal. I put the boots on, went home. I loved those boots.

We were eating supper. A knock came on the kitchen door. There stood Tony and his dad. They had the tire. I had done nothing wrong, but it didn't look good for me. My dad and Tony's dad went outside and talked. When my daddy came back in the kitchen, Mother was still sitting at the table. Dad looked at me. He said I would have to give Tony back his boots. He would give me the tire back. I did. I got the best deal trading. I sure did love those boots. What a time I had. Love to trade stuff.

Thanks for my mom and daddy for this. They gave me my freedom to do this.

I have a pair of rubber boots from L.L. Bean. Even when I put them on, I still think of Seco, KY. With memories of the tire and boot trade. Tony was a woosie. Couldn't stand the bad trade but that was alright. I could make a bad trade or deal and live with it.

I am still doing this. Make little, lose a little. Make more than you. Lose. Profit. Profit. Thanks Seco, KY. Love you.

Chapter Twenty-Four

Gary Hooper— Script Trading

I will start with the truth about Gary Hooper. He was sorta different. Know what I mean. He was one of the guys who liked to dress different. One day, he wanted to ride my pony. He gave me a bag of script (some coins the miners would use to buy goods at the company store). We traded. He rode my pony, which was named Spot—white. Gary rode him for a while. I didn't know what I had in the bag, but I thought it was a good trade.

I took the bag of script to Mr. Preston. He was the big man in Seco, KY. He looked at the bag of script—or money and asked me where I got this. I told him. He gave me a pretty good amount of money for the script. He said it was always good as money. I don't know how much he gave me for the exchange. I probably bought baseballs or something.

I know Gary Hooper will go to Heaven or has gone.

His father, don't know his first name, as we were taught to call the men of your senior by their last name. Mr. Hooper was all I knew him by. Mr. Hooper was a dignified man. Always wore a suit and tie.

Mr. Hooper, you were a man of distinction. Probably was something to make what I am today. Thank you very much. I know you are in Heaven today. I will see you someday.

Chapter Twenty-Five
The Trains—
Mr. Hooper

Mr. Hooper had a big house with a basement. He had trains on tables. They were everywhere. This was a most wonderful thing to see. He knew how to do this stuff—smoke, lights. Must have 5 or more trains running at the same time.

I wonder what has happened to all of his most valuable and most cherished possessions. Who knows.

I sure did like to see all the trains, bridges, tunnels, smoke, lights and whistles. Thank you again, Mr. Hooper. You will go to Heaven.

Chapter Twenty-Six
Mr. Ora Spears

Mr. Spears was a most wonderful man. He always wore a suit and tie, very clean. Very well groomed.

As I remember, Mr. Spears was on the road waiting for a ride (on the main road) going to Neon or somewhere. A car hit him and killed him. What a tragedy. He was a most humble person. He was raised in an orphanage and got educated, came to Seco, KY and got a job, raised a family, got killed. What a life.

Mr. Ora Spears, I will never forget you. You are a very big part of my life. I will see you in Heaven someday.

Dewey was his son. We grew up together. Dewey was working for the store in Seco. One day, he and Big Foot Hall (that's what they called him) were delivering groceries on a truck. They were going out of Seco and had to cross a railroad track with no bells or lights. As they were getting near the tracks, they didn't know how close the train was to them. The train struck the truck. I guess the train hit the truck as it crossed the tracks. The train engine pushed the truck quite a ways. Big Foot Hall was the driver of the truck. Dewey was helping him deliver the groceries. Big Foot was killed in the wreck. Dewey lost part of his ear. We heard about this while in lunch at school. Dewey survived this tragic wreck but Big Foot didn't. He was killed. His daddy came running, running down to the road. Screaming, crying, "My son, my son. The Sam, the Sam." That was his son's name, whom was dead.

I don't know what ever happened to Sam's dad. They lived in Whitaker, a little town next to Seco. I am sure he grieved a lot after that tragic day.

Dewey recovered from the accident, went to college. Don't know much after that.

This is just another day in Seco, KY. Always something different. Never knowing what was going to happen next.

This was, and still is, my favorite little place—Seco, KY.

Chapter Twenty-Seven
Cod Liver Oil

The famous cure for everything. When I was very young—between maybe four and ten—I was sick a lot. Had colds, bronchial pneumonia, sore throat, earaches. My mother apparently believed the famous cod liver oil was the cure for illness. She started feeding this every morning—one big tablespoon every morning. I would get out of bed, get dressed, go downstairs, walk to the kitchen table, pick up the big spoon, pour this Godforsaken, greasy, awful-smelling, brown stuff into the spoon and put in my mouth.

This was a ritual to me every morning. Get up, go downstairs, take this greasy spoon, drink this smelly fish oil and eat your oatmeal or a cream of wheat, toast, butter and eggs. My mom always fixed a good, warm breakfast before going to play or going to school. I guess this is why I eat a lot of fish to this day. My mom said it is good for your bones and everything else. What can I say, at this writing she is now 100 years of age and I'm 71 years of age. there must be something to this great and wonderful stuff.

This wonderful stuff my mom called cod liver oil. If you drink a tablespoon every day, you will live to be old. Famous words from the wise.

I was my mom's third and last child. Favorite she says. I know she kept me as close to her as she could. What a wonderful person and a Christian person. If she does not go to Heaven to be with the Lord, then no man nor woman will be there.

Last words about this wonderful stuff—cod liver oil. Believe it or not, I still take it and have a bottle of the tablets in the cabinet with my blood pressure medicine. Thanks, Mom. When I take one of the tablets, I think of you. I love you.

What a life in Seco, KY.

If you have not taken cod liver oil, you should.

Chapter Twenty-Eight
Smoking Corn Silks

The gang was always doing things. Don't know how we came to do the things we did.

Corn silks—this was the hairy looking stuff that came off the corn. It told you when the corn was ready to pull off the stalk. Don't know how we started smoking this stuff, but we did.

We would take some corn silk (looked like black hair, weird looking stuff) and put it in a piece of brown paper bag which we got from home. It looked like a cigarette. Wasn't quite as perfect. Don't know why or how all this came about but it sure was good. The paper would burn at first, then go out. Don't know where the matches came from.

We would sit together. I would roll a smoke, something pretty long. more like a cigar. I would light it. The paper would burn a little until it got to the silk. It would go out. You would take a big breath in. Very strong, burned your throat. We would pass these things around. Got pretty buzzed on this. Maybe the corn silk or maybe the paper. We got pretty dizzy. Probably breathing in so deep.

We could only do this once a year. This tells you we didn't do this much. Probably good. We would have been corn silk addicts.

Recently, I saw a cornfield beside the road. I stopped at the time the corn was ready to pick. I stole a few corncobs and brought them home. Rolled me a big corn silk cigar. I mean big.

It was hotter than Hell. Burned my throat. Tasted good even in a paper bag from Kroger's store. Same as Seco, KY grocery store. Got a pretty big buzz.

What a place to live. If my parents had only known. My mother thought I was an angel. I was! Seco was my Heaven. Didn't need anything else. Still don't need much. I still live in the woods, looking at a lake, birds, deer, fox, rabbits.

Chapter Twenty-Nine
Rabbit Tobacco

I don't know where this stuff got its name. All I heard was the rabbits would shit on this certain plant. The leaves would turn gray or white. You could see rabbit shit next to the plant. We would smoke this stuff. Not the shit but the leaves. Don't know for sure, maybe either one. We would smoke this stuff pretty good. We could get pretty high. Maybe a buzz.

The only time you could get this stuff was in the fall. Cold weather, which I didn't like at all. We would search for this stuff. Wasn't very much to find, but what we found was good. I can still taste this, sorta strong but a very good flavor. Can't describe it. Wish I could find some. One good puff and you got pretty dizzy. Sometimes, we would also chew this rabbit tobacco. Had to get it pretty moist before you could get a flavor. I cannot describe this either. Pretty good chew for nothing. Didn't have to buy Beechnut tobacco or Brown Mule, Apple, Mammoth Cave twist. Maybe someday when I get to Heaven, the Lord will pass a little bit of rabbit tobacco to chew. Who knows. Heaven might be a pretty good place to live for us little boys who grew up in Seco, KY. I know God took good care of us or I would not be writing this for you to read. The Devil didn't have a chance because we were probably meaner than him. He was in Hell and we were in Heaven in Seco,

Ky. with our Lord Jesus Christ. He guarded us with a guardian angel all of the time.

This was a wonderful time in my little town of Seco, KY. No worries, not like today. Didn't need McDonalds, Dunkin Donuts. Just a little bit of rabbit chew. Sure would like a little chew now, but I do have my pipe. Think I will have one before my next chapter. Maybe a sip of cherry pie.

Chapter Thirty
Funerals—Food—Satan

I think the first person I ever saw dead in a casket was my great grandfather—my mother's mother's father. I could not have been but a little boy. It was in Bottom Fork where my mother now lives. They did their own ways—no embalming—or that is what I know now. They washed the person, dressed them, put them in a coffin. They did this in the house where my mother now lives.

I remember him laying in the hallway of the house. I was barely able to see him in the coffin. He had a big beard, very nice looking and dressed nice. My great grandmother was also put the same way.

I remember when she died, probably a hundred years or close. I wasn't there but they took her from her bedroom after she died. But before they took her out of the bedroom, they washed and dressed her in her black dress—white collar and all pretty. This was a few years later after her husband died. These people lived a long time. At this writing, my mother is 100 years and six months old. What a life. She has gone through 20 presidents or more. I now sleep in the bedroom where these people died. Not many or none will sleep in this bedroom, because of the things that happen in this bedroom. I will get back to these things later about the ghosts of Bottom Fork; another book!

Chapter Thirty-One
The Food and Satanic Ritual

It seemed to be a big food thing about death. They would eat and eat after burial. I didn't like it then, don't like it now. Very satanic. Why would you want to eat after a death? Seems crazy to me. I guess a free meal. Maybe to some people, this was their best meal when someone died. They might not even know who the dead person was. If they heard of someone that died, find out where they live, go look at the body, shake a hand or two, find the food. Eat a little of all they have. Whoever it was, I know not. What a meal. After people ate, they would sit around all over the place. Don't know why they hung around so long—too full to leave—I guess. Some of them would even go to sleep. People would finally leave— one Hell of a mess to clean up. They needed a Golden Corral—hog trough.

Know what I mean? When I die, no food. Just whiskey, beer, nuts, pretzels, salami, cheese. Party. Go home. Go to bed. Be happy. I am in Heaven.

Chapter Thirty-Two
Winter Time in Seco, KY

What a time! It would snow a lot in the winter time. It seemed like it anyway. I never did like snow. Still don't.

We had sleds with blades on them. We got them at the company store. They were Western Flyers. You could guide them with the bars on front of the sled. It was cold and we would build a big fire using tires the Coal Company would give us. The snow was deep and very cold. Number One Holler was the best place to sleigh ride. Probably a mile of very fast riding.

One night, Kyle Reach was on a sleigh. He was flying down the holler, solid ice. Probably going 50 m.p.h. He ran off the road, hit a concrete drain wall and broke his leg. He had a crooked leg the rest of his life.

Winter time was beautiful in Seco, KY. Building snow men, sleigh riding, fires, roasting marshmallows, trying to stay warm. We would ride our sleighs day and night. We would go home to eat something warm or hot—usually soup, crackers, bologna sandwiches. Then we would get dressed with all you could put on and still walk. It was a long walk back to the starting place, at least a mile—very steep. At night, everyone was there. Parents of us, everyone in town seemed like. The parents would ride one time. They could double ride. The dads would get on the sled first. Then the moms would get on top of him.

Someone would start pushing the sled. Getting them going fast. Us kids would not see them again. We would do this until we were so tired and the fire was going out. I would go home to my place I loved. This was my whole world. My mom and dad, my bed, and my bedroom. Roy Rogers, Gene Autry, Whip Wilson, Hopalong Cassidy, Lash Larue, Tim Holt, Red Ryder and many more on one of the walls of my bedroom. Bed cover and all.

As a boy in Seco, KY, you didn't worry about someone breaking into your house or hurting you. Just go to bed living a peaceful day and night—going to sleep, not a fear at all. Waking up in Heaven and doing it again today. Having breakfast—Cream of Wheat, hot biscuits and butter, lots of butter in the Cream of Wheat, milk, sugar, a very big bowl, two fried eggs, apple butter and butter on the biscuits. Get ready to go sleigh riding again.

I can't remember his name but once we were sleigh riding and he was flying on the sleigh. He hit the railroad track, very sharp edge. He cut his head and face very bad. Didn't look good for a long time. This was what it was in my small world of Seco, KY in the wintertime. Every day was a new world, never knowing what was going to happen until it did. Didn't matter. I lived every moment to the highest point. Still do. Live your life to the highest level possible.

Thanks to my mom and dad for taking care of me so good.

What a life for a little boy in a little town in a little world of Seco, KY.

Chapter Thirty-Three

Train Rides to Grandparents in Whick, KY

As I begin to write this chapter, I am sitting here smoking my pipe, 71 years old. My mother is in the hospital—She is 100 years plus. Don't know if she will make it till this book is finished. She is with my family on Christmas, wife, my daughters, great grand kids. Not this year. But we will see her. Love you, Mom. Miss you.

My Papaw, as I called him, and my Mamaw, as I called her, lived in Whick, KY in Breatitt County. Probably never heard of this place. I was just a little boy in Seco, KY, who loved them. The only way you could get to Whick, KY was by train. I know this seems strange, but true.

I would visit them as soon as school was out—couldn't wait. My mom and dad would get things worked out with them (when I was going to be there) by letters. The train was my transportation there.

The L&N Railroad ran the tracks to I didn't know where, but I knew I would get to my Papaw and Mamaw. They would put me on the train early in the morning—passenger train—beautiful. I had plenty of food: chicken, biscuits, peanut butter sandwich, cookies.

They would kiss me goodbye. I was off on an adventure. I loved it. Didn't matter to me, wasn't scared. Probably 8-9 years old, maybe less. I would sit in the most beautiful seats, soft, big, wide. The train would start turning, the coal made the power. It would sound like chug, chug, chug. Move faster until smooth.

I would sit there, no people on the train. This is where the trip started. Still dark. The coach or car would rock back and forth. Felt good. I loved it. Looking out the window—houses, people, trees. There was a man on the train called the conductor. He was a very nice man. He dressed nice, black suit, gold buttons on this coat (jacket), a nice hat like a captain's and a gold watch chain that you could see. He would look at the watch often, making sure the train was on schedule. He walked through the aisle of the passenger car and asked for your ticket, you handed it to him and he would stamp it. You were paid up—ready to ride. It was dark, but you could see people and stuff.

I probably slept a little, early morning, daylight, very bright. All you could hear were the train tracks, click, click, the train engines, the movement of the passenger car. What a beautiful room of seats. Red color it was.

The conductor would come through the car and tell you where we were. The train would stop, pick up people. They would step on. People would have chickens, pigs, bags of feed. Hogs that were dead, halves of them. Cleaned, clean, ready to cook or whatever.

They would put all this stuff on the racks above them. I would sit and watch. I loved this stuff. People would open their baskets. They had food. Plenty! They had biscuits, chicken, bacon. All kinds of stuff. Never offered me any. Most of them didn't look too clean anyway. Didn't have much I guess. There weren't many roads. The railroad was the main way to travel. Many towns the railroad was the only access. The train would stop at some stations.

Mules, wagons, horses, men and women waiting for the families or things they had ordered.

What a trip this is.

I had a big basket my mom had fixed. Biscuits with sausage, biscuits with apple butter. More food than I could eat.

There was a toilet on the passenger car, in the rear. I had to pee. I got in, closed the door. Stood there over the toilet. I could see the ground below me moving fast. I realized whatever you did went on the ground below. Pee or poop. I did pee. Pretty funny watching your pee fly somewhere. I loved it. I can still see gravels on the tracks below. I would go back and sit down. The car would rock back and forth. The tracks going click, click, clack. The trees, people, mules and wagons. Smell the coal smoke from the engine, powered by steam and coal. Smelled good to me. This is how my house was heated, coal. This is how my daddy made a living for my family and me. Coal.

I would eat something while I was looking out the window thinking about my Papaw and Mamaw waiting for me at the railroad station. I would get up, go to the water cabinet. It looked like a cabinet; had big jug of water in the middle of it, cup you pulled out of a little tube—pull a little handle and water ran into your cup. It was cold, good water. I miss my little town. I miss my mommy a lot and Daddy. I know she was missing me. I would go back and sit down in the big seat. Take a nap I guess. Long trip.

Again, the train would stop many times. Every little town. The train was the only way for a lot of people to get their goods: clothes, food, things for Christmas. Some of them looked pretty poor. The kids looked pretty bad, barefoot, not clean. Probably still like this. The train would begin pulling out. Smoke, smell of coal, slow moving, picking up speed. Rocking back and forth. I was on my way again to my Papaw and Mamaw's house.

The conductor would come around walking down the aisle of the passenger car, which was full of people. He carried a big box with a strap around his neck to hold the box. He had candy, gum, Cracker Jacks, Chicklets. The Chicklets were Liquorets. Black outside and inside. I would buy them. They were a nickel. Big box. One nickel could buy this. The conductor would call out each by name. It was like a song the way he did it. He was a handsome man, now gone to Heaven.

I probably slept a lot on the train. Chickens would cackle, pigs would oink. Lots of noise. People eating while traveling to where they were going. Some clean and some not so clean. I actually saw a woman get an egg from one of the hen chickens.

Finally, the conductor, walking down the aisle of the car, was calling the name of the train station, which he did all the way. He called the name "Whick, Whick. We are approaching Whick, KY." I couldn't wait to see my Papaw and Mamaw. I must stop here for a moment—

I have the most wonderful grandson in the world. He reminds me so much of me. He loves to visit with me and his Gran. Just like I did with mine. My Pap and Mamaw didn't have much at all at the time. Food, visiting with me on the big porch, no radio, no T.V. Just us three and love for each other. No computers, no I-pods. We do have a T.V. Ha. And games, but Cal, our grandson enjoys just being with us. Laid back, no big deal. Whatever happens happens. That was how it was in Whick, KY with my grandparents. This is how it is with us three in Lancaster, KY on beautiful Harrington Lake in the woods overlooking the water. What a life. Thanks Cal for being what, and who, you are. Thanks for the boat rides, swimming with me across the lake many times. So many memories I can't write all of them. I know you know all of them. I love you so much, my Buddy. God was good when He gave me you as my grandson.

Back to my book:

Pap and Mamaw were waiting for me. Pap had a wagon with two mules that pulled it. Jim and Jack were their names. Pap put me in the middle of the seat and off we would go to their house (which was a long way). We would go through a big tunnel, under the railroad track then across the Kentucky River in the wagon. Water would get on your feet but we would make it across. We would finally get home. I love it. Very simple: wood stove, no electricity, lamps at night, fireplaces, warm beds (feather beds). Loved them.

My Mamaw cooked on the wood-burning stove. My meal in the evening was chicken, potatoes, cornbread, green beans, homemade butter and molasses. Pap would take molasses, stir the butter and put this on the cornbread. It was good, real good. Go to bed early—with the chickens. You covered up with the feather bed blanket, a lot of cover. The fireplaces would go out—might be cold. Wake up in the morning and Mamaw had the biscuits ready. She would then fix eggs, gravy, homemade butter with molasses, home made bacon, sausage. Everything was home grown or homemade. Not much store bought. Smelled as good as it tasted. My Pap would pray for a long time it seemed. He was a preacher.

We would eat. Good stuff. There was a picture hanging on the wall, this old man praying. He had bread and soup, his hands together, giving thanks for what he had. I always wanted that picture but didn't get it. Later, I found one that is now hanging in my barber shop. I have had it probably 30-35 years. It is called "Grace". We should all give thanks for what we have. Amen. Thank you, Jesus, for my being born.

I will take a short break to smoke my pipe.

As I said, my Papaw was a preacher. On Sunday morning, we would get up, have a big breakfast and get dressed to go to church. My Pap would dress in his best—white shirt, no tie, collar buttoned, brown pants. He had on his best shoes, shined, lace-ups. He was a very handsome man, no beard nor mustache, short hair. I loved him very much. Still do. I miss him a lot same as my dad.

We walked to church. He would not work his mules on the weekend. They rested. Sabbath day. We walked one or two miles. I walked behind him. He had a big Bible in his hand. Didn't say a word. I didn't mind. I was happy to be with my Papaw. We finally got to the little church. Not big at all. Maybe 50 people at most. Maybe 20 to 23 people were there. I think it was a Holiness or Pentecostal. My Pap would preach and preach and preach. People would shout a lot. He would say funny words. Didn't know at the time, but found out years later they called it 'Speaking in Tongues'. I liked it. Pretty cool. We would leave to go back to our house. I probably should have been a preacher or snake handler. Ha.

My Mamaw didn't go with us. Maybe too far for her to walk. I know she was a very religious woman. Prayed a lot. I know she is in Heaven today. She was so beautiful. I can still smell her body aroma. Never have, nor every again will I have, the aroma of her. I loved her so much. She is in Heaven with my Pap and my daddy. I miss them all.

When we got home, my Mamaw had dinner ready. Cornbread, green beans, pork or some kind of meat. Lots of other stuff. Didn't do much all day. Pap didn't do anything on Sunday. Sabbath day. I played doing whatever; chasing chickens, wading in the creek (very cold), watching the hogs roll in the mud, smelled really bad. Pap had a big horse. He would put his Buena Vista saddle on him or her. Don't know which. Doesn't matter. I would ride and ride.

Pap and Mamaw had a big porch, wood, of course. Pap would let me drill with his bit and drill. I would drill holes in the big porch. He didn't care.

Mamaw had very long hair, down to her waist. In the evening, we would sit on the big porch. I would sit in her lap in a big rocking chair. She smelled so good. She sure loved me. I loved her, too. Still do. I miss her memories. Mamaw would take the hair pins out of her hair, let it fall. Very long. She let me brush her hair. It was longer than I was tall. I brushed her hair until it was easy to brush. She knew when to stop brushing. Then she would put it back up in a bun.

After one big Sunday, the chickens were going to the trees to roost for the night. Don't know why they sleep in trees. Probably to stay away from animals and such. This is when you get ready to go to bed. Maybe a little popcorn or molasses cookies. Mamaw made everything. The cookies were very good. I do really good baking them—taste a lot like hers. The popcorn wasn't Orville's popcorn. This was real popcorn. Pap raised the corn, let it dry out, take it off the cobb. Mamaw would put this in a big pot, put it on the coals in the fireplace. Coals very hot. It would pop. Didn't have too much salt, no butter, just popcorn. Tasted good then. No Coke or root beer, just plain water. Loved it. Still do. Gone to bed—good night.

Must tell you this. Talked to my mom this morning in the nursing home. Not doing well at all. She is very weak, talking very low. In her loving voice says she is fine. She is so precious to me. I hate to let her go, but I am ready. No need for her to linger for she is going to be with the rest of her loved ones in Heaven. Sorry for the delay, but I though I would let you know how she was doing. Thanks.

Chapter Thirty-Four
My Dog Pete

Pete was my favorite dog. He was a Shepherd, Collie mix (I was told). Blonde collar, long nose, light brown body. Beautiful dog and very loving and close to me. He was always by my side. Got him when he was a pup. Don't know why I named him Pete. Sounded good. Maybe short for religious reason—Peter. He sure took care of me. Some man in the Bible. My mommy couldn't begin to scold me. Pete knew it, much less spank me. He would growl at her and that didn't go very well with my dad. Pete also protected our house. We lived in Seco, but outside of town, this man was selling Bibles. My daddy told him if he could get to our front door, he would buy a Bible. Knock came on our door. Here stood this man. My daddy bought a Bible. Dad asked how he did this without being bitten by Pete. The man told dad Pete met him wagging his tail. Pete must have been a Baptist or Methodist like me.

Pete didn't like black people for some reason. Don't know why. Every time one would walk up the road, Pete was running after them. My daddy did not like this. That is when Dad decided to take Pete to Papaw in Whick, KY. From that day, the only time I got to see him was when I went to see my Pap and Mamaw. Pete always knew when I was coming. He was waiting for me at the station. Pete got old, skinny. I have a picture somewhere of me and Pete. I guess Pap buried him. Don't know where. Pete is in Heaven with Pap and Mamaw. Never doubt in your mind that there is not a Heaven for animals. What carried the Virgin Mary, the mother of Jesus?! Good thought.

Chapter Thirty-Five
Reunions at Bottom Fork

Born in Seco, KY didn't mean no other place existed, particularly Bottom Fork, KY. This is where Mom's family started, her grandfather.

Never did like reunions, went because I had to. Old people who met once a year with their kids, their kids, their kids. From everywhere, Ohio, Virginia, N.C., S.C., W.Va. I sure didn't care. My mother now lives in the house where all of this happened. Her grandfather built the house.

The day of the reunion, they would bring all the families out to take pictures—oldest, of course. Five or more generations. Lived a long time as I said. Me, my mother, her mother—plus the men; my Great Grandmother (it seemed she was always in bed). They would bring her out to take pictures once a year.

It was time. My God how time goes by. Another reunion. Holy shit! I thought.

Daddy got up early to go to Bottom Fork to help Uncle Jim get things ready—tables and all. Daddy didn't know what was in store for him. This is how he told the happening to me.

When he got to Great Grandmother's house, he went in, things were fine. Uncle Jim's daughter and boyfriend were there. Uncle Jim came to the door; his daughter and boyfriend got under the bed in the house. Uncle Jim had a gun with him. Dad knew there was going to be trouble. He went out the back door and hid in the big chicken house. He heard shots from guns. Didn't know what was happening.

Uncle Jim was mad that his daughter was marrying him. Uncle Jim was in the house looking for them, knew they were in the house. He started shooting under the beds. He shot his daughter's boyfriend. Didn't know at the time. He went outside and saw Daddy. He told dad to go to the chicken house and stay in there and if you come out I will kill you. Dad knew this. Someone came up in a car to help. Uncle Jim told him to leave. When he tried to get in his car, Uncle Jim fired his gun. The man started running down the road. Uncle Jim shot the man in the back and killed him.

He accidentally shot his son in the neck, didn't die. My grandmother fell and broke her arm. What a day at Bottom Fork. Uncle Jim went to the woods. Dad came out of the chicken house. Got help. There was no reunion at Bottom Fork today. They took his son to Seco Hospital and his daughter's boyfriend. Both survived.

Two or three days later, at night, a knock came on our front door. It was Uncle Jim with his rifle. He gave it to Dad. Dad got the police. Uncle Jim wanted to see his son in the hospital. They took him there. Never saw him again for years. Sent him to prison, very fast. When my grandmother passed away, who do you think was at her funeral? Uncle Jim. He was in the last pew in the church. When the service was over, he was gone. I have never seen him again, nor has anyone.

Uncle Jim was a fine man, husband, father. I guess he got pissed off. Didn't want his daughter to marry this guy. What is the old saying—shit happens. They did get married. Probably still are.

This was the way it was told. To believe—I know.

They had many more reunions. I guess. Didn't go to many. Didn't like them, still don't My mommy is the last one standing. Don't know how much longer this will last. This is how it was for a little boy in Seco, KY. What a life. Great memories. Thanks, Mom. I love you.

Chapter Thirty-Six
Poison Ivy

Poison ivy was the worst thing that could happen to you, and I was the one that was attracted to it. There were more than me, but it was Hell. We all played on the rocks where the poison ivy was. Didn't think or care. We would slide and play. Poison ivy everywhere. All I had to do was look at it. I got it. I would get big blisters on my fingers and feet so bad. I would cry, itch, scratch. Pink Calamine Lotion was the best thing for it. I got it so bad. Dr. Wright put me under the heat lamps in the hospital surgery room. He would take big scissors and burst the blisters. Then put this purple liquid on them. Felt good.

Dickie Craft, my first cousin, would get it so bad my other first cousin, Jimmy Craft, would sit with him and feed him ice cream. Eyes closed, swollen body with poison ivy. Milkshakes were his favorite. he could suck through a straw. Seems he was pink all over his body. Dickie died, a very deadly disease called Hunting's Corea. Family genes. Maybe more on this later. Don't know.

Anyway, so much about poison ivy. Bad stuff. This is just another day in Seco, KY. I have not had poison ivy in a long time. What a place to live. Maybe a little itch would feel good. Sure do miss my little town.

Talked to Mom today, not doing too good in the nursing home.

Taking a break, my pipe and a sip of cherry pie.

Cherry pie is a mixture of cherries and moonshine. I make my own. Take a quart jar. Fill with cherries, about 2/3 of a quart. Fill the rest with moonshine. The longer it sits, the better it is. This moonshine is probably 100 or more proof. Doesn't take much. A couple of good sips and you know it.

I get my moonshine from a man in Estill County. Don't know his name or where he lives. I meet him. Doesn't say much, does his business and on his way. So much about cherry pie.

Chapter Thirty-Seven
The Motor Barn

Southeast Coal Company—better known as Seco, had lots of machinery. One of the buildings was where they kept their heavy motor cars. The cars were huge, made from iron and steel. I mean <u>Big</u>. They ran off of electricity. Lots of power. More volts than I could even imagine. The big electric cables ran all through the mines, miles and miles of this. Us boys, the gang, would go to the motor barn on weekends, when no one was there. I could handle these big monsters pretty well for a little boy. You would put the big pole with the copper tip on the Electric line, depending on which way you wanted to go. Live wires. The seat was hard. You had a steering wheel with a knob on it. This was the power control. Someone had to switch the tracks to move out of the barn. We would do this for a couple of hours; get bored and move on to something else. The good Lord and many guardian angels were with us all the time. We were very religious.

We could have gotten run over by one of these big motors or killed from the electric current. These machines probably weighed 30 to 50 tons. They were huge.

This one they called the buggy. It was small, easy to handle. One day, I was running one pretty fast and ran out of track. Not good. I didn't get hurt—I jumped off and wrecked the buggy. They never knew who did this. I sure didn't want to go to Greendale—a jail for boys in Lexington, KY. We probably did things to warrant us going. Lucky, never got caught. We spent a lot of hours on the motors, knew a lot about them. Sure do wish you could have seen them. So big, so powerful. Most were painted yellow and orange. I guess the company had their own colors.

My daddy was a motorman. One day, they brought a new motor machine to town. This thing was huge. I mean huge. Must have been 30 feet long. They gave it to my dad to operate. He was proud of this monster. It would pull many coal cars from inside the mines. This is what he did. I did get to ride with him a few times. You could feel the power from the big machine.

Another time in a little boy's life in Seco, KY. Wish you could have been there. What a wonderful experience this was. Wouldn't trade it for anything. Our gang was lucky, none of us lost our lives. Thank the Lord for this. We were all angels in His eyes. He took good care of us. What a job he had. He slept good I bet. Laughed a lot at us.

I can still smell the coal and oil from the big motors. Loved it. What a hard job our daddies had. Thanks, Dad, for everything you gave me: my life. Love you. Didn't have you long enough.

Chapter Thirty-Eight
Weenie—My Little Pig

How does a little boy remember so much. Didn't realize this until I decided to write about my part of life in Seco, KY. Not very important to most, but to me, it was a major part.

Daddy, Mom and I went to Pine Mountain to have a wiener roast. There was a place you could go to have a picnic. I guess Daddy built a little fire. We had hot dogs with wieners. Got finished. When we started down Pine Mountain, Daddy was driving. Dark. I saw something running down the road. Looked like a pup or something. I asked Daddy to stop. He did. I got out of the car and caught this little pig. No bigger than my little hand. Got in the back seat. Mommie asked me what I had. I told her it was a little pig. We got home. I had a little pig and didn't know what to do with it.

Daddy put it in the out building where we kept coal and stuff. I guess he put it in a box or something.

The next morning, I went to check on it. I picked it up, white and pink skin. I brought it in the house. Mom got a bottle and nipple (baby bottle), put some milk in it and gave it to me to feed the little pig. It took it like a little baby would. It drank until full.

I named the little pig Weenie for the weenie roast me, Mommie and Daddy had on Pine Mountain. Weenie grew, ate anything I fed her. Didn't know Weenie was a she pig. She grew out of the out building. She loved me. She was like a dog, followed me around. She grew into a big pig. Moved her to a place on Number One Holler, they called it.

I would go around town in the morning and get food for her. I put buckets on people's porches and they would put their food scraps in my bucket. I would take this and feed Weenie. She had a lot of food to eat. Probably should have taken it home. Made good soup. Ha.

Weenie grew into a hog. Still my pet. Loved me.

One day, Daddy told me Weenie was going to have some babies. How could this happen? She was with other hogs. Probably with some pretty pigs, male, of course. I guess that's why they call the male hogs, female sows.

Weenie was pregnant, not married. Probably didn't know the daddy of her babies. Same as today.

Weenie finally had her babies—seven of them. They were very little. Black and white, all of them. They all lived, they loved their mommie. I would watch them nurse and sleep on Weenie, their mommie. They grew and grew into little pigs, like their mommie did.

The little guys and gals grew up. Daddy said I would probably sell them. I didn't want to do that, seven pigs, but I did. Sold them for $10 a piece. Pretty good. Probably bought baseball stuff. Gave the rest to Mom and Dad. As long as I had a baseball glove, bat, ball and my bike. I didn't need anything else.

Fall of the year was coming. Daddy said it was time to get Weenie fat for killing. Didn't want this to happen, but it was okay. Weenie was ready for the winter eatery at our house.

Thanks Weenie for being a part of my life in our little town of Seco, KY. I still think of you running down the road on Pine Mountain. Lots of time when eating bacon, sausage, I think of my little Weenie. Thanks.

Chapter Thirty-Nine
Camping Out—Log House

Camping out was a big part of our lives in Seco, KY.

In the summer, we would spend more time in the woods than at home it seemed. Probably not. When you are a little boy, you think different.

We would take a blanket, plenty of food. Our moms would fix plenty of stuff: wieners, peanut butter, crackers and leftovers from whatever they could find for us to eat. When it got dark, we would build a fire. You could hear owls, coyotes, birds. Sounded pretty scary sometimes. We would sit around the fire, eating and listening to all the sounds. Talked about what we were going to do in the morning. We would wake up chilly. Didn't take long to get going. Eat the same thing. We would try to dress like Indians. Did pretty good too.

The man in the machine shop gave us some plastic that was used in mines. It was yellow, heavy plastic, more like rubber. We would make something that looked like diapers. Indian stuff. Mixed mud and berries, put on our faces. Find turtle shells and drink water to make you a real Indian. Pretty tough stuff for us guys. We would play until ready to go home again, planning our next great adventure in the wild.

Chapter Forty
Log House

This log house was built by South East Coal Company in Seco, KY. I guess for the big shots of the mining company. They stopped using it, so us boys of Seco began to use it for camping out. We would go up on the hill where it was. Had a big fireplace. We would gather firewood for a big night. There were probably 10-12 of us boys. We would take enough food for many people.

All of us had dogs, they would go with us to protect us from all the Indians or whatever came around. We would sit around the big fireplace and roast marshmallows, wieners, beans. We took our water in big gallon jugs. They were glass. Guess there wasn't plastic. One of the jugs was empty, no more water in it. Jimmy Jones broke my jug—my jug. I hit him with a rock and cut his head. Not bad. Bled a little. He was older but not as tough as me. I could throw as straight as a major league pitcher. Still can.

We finally went to bed, laying in front of the big fireplace. We were all passing gas or farting from all the beans and stuff. Even the dogs moved around or went outside. Can't remember who went outside to use the woods as a toilet. More than one for sure. Lots of beans, I guess, water, marshmallows. Sounds awful—it was. I guess all of us pooped a lot.

We were in bed, covered up with our blankets, didn't know what was beginning to happen. The dogs were outside. Don't know how many, but one of them or all had followed us to poop. Dogs will eat what tastes good, I guess.

We were laying down. One of the dogs had eaten a lot of poop, came in the cabin and laid down beside Billy, breathing in his face. He jumped up and said, "His breath smells like shit." Which it was. We all laughed a lot at this. Finally, we all settled down, dogs and all beside their buddies—and Billy and his.

Woke up the next morning. Ready to fix some eggs or whatever we had to eat.

The big log house was a big and beautiful place to go to anytime. Not many people even knew it was there, way back in the woods. We spent many nights there. I can still smell the logs burning, beans, marshmallows, popcorn. I guess the dogs are still eating poop. We had some pretty smart dogs. Our best friends—still are.

I miss these most wonderful days of my life. But what a life. The log house was burned down by someone, but the memories still linger.

Thanks for the log cabin in Seco, KY. Thanks for my God for taking care of me and my buddies in the most wonderful times of our lives. What a life in the little town of Seco, KY. Thanks.

Chapter Forty-One
Yellow Houses—
Painting by the Men—
All the Same Color in Seco, KY

I didn't know then why they painted everything in Seco, KY yellow—still don't. Good buy on paint, I guess.

The grocery store building housed all the business to do with the coal company. The grocery store was on the left side when you went in, on the right side was dry goods—clothes, shoes, glassware, material for women to buy to make clothes for the family.

Lena Proffit was in charge of the material and stuff. She was a very nice person and very pretty. Always kind to all of us boys.

Chapter Forty-Two
Company Store

The company store housed a lot. It was painted bright yellow. On the top front was painted in black—S.E.C.O., South East Coal Company. The barber shop was next to it, also painted yellow. Across the road was the post office, restaurant, theatre. And upstairs was the hospital, all in one building. Also painted yellow. Every house, I mean, every damn one of them. The Bottom, Number One Holler, Number Two Holler, Hatcher Hill, Boss Hill. Thinking now, why didn't they paint the streets yellow. They also painted the outdoor toilets yellow.

I can still see the men that painted the houses. They did this every spring, warm weather, late spring, early summer, I guess. These men had big nails in the sides of the houses. They would put hangers on the nails, then big boards. They would climb up on the boards with buckets of paint and brushes. They would paint as far as they could reach. They did this every day until they got the houses and everything else painted. They would go somewhere else to paint, I guess. Only saw them once a year. I will try to find out why they painted all of Seco, KY. yellow. There had to be a reason.

Chapter Forty-Three
Halloween

Halloween was a big thing in Seco, KY. It wasn't as big as Christmas, but pretty close.

The gang had plans the first night; we turned the toilet's house over. Hard to do, but we did it. Can't tell her name, she was sitting on the toilet seat when the outhouse went over. There she was on the stool. She stood up, never saw a woman in the partial nude. We all ran like hell. She didn't see us but we saw her. May she rest in peace. I know she's in Heaven. She was a Christian woman, mother, wife. Thank you for a look at you in your flesh. we (the gang) talked about you for awhile.

Mr. Williams was a fine man. We took a bag of poop—put it on his porch, lit it and knocked on his door. When he came to the door, it was burning. He stomped to put out the fire, of course. He had shit all over his shoes. We hid behind a big tree and watched him. He went back into his house. We didn't know, but he came out the back door with his shotgun, loaded. He sneaked in behind us boys and fired his shotgun right behind us. Scared us to near death. He laughed about it. He probably had the best trick of all.

We went to the school. They had outdoor toilets there too. There was a walk of wood to the toilets. We turned the toilets over. The gang probably would have gone to Greendale for this crime. it was in Lexington, KY. This was a place for boys who did crimes. My daddy always said, if you do anything bad, you would go to

Greendale. It scared you to be good. Didn't go there. Lucky, I guess.

We went to the road that the cars drove on. We put a big log across the road. We laid down on the bank. A car came down the road and hit the log. We ran away. Don't know how much damage was done to the car. We all would have been sent to Greendale. Thank you, Lord, for taking care of us. We all had a guardian angel to protect us. I know I did.

We did many other things on this night, got plenty of treats. What a life in Seco, KY.

Chapter Forty-Four
Rocks and Trains

Trains were a big part of my life and the gang's life in Seco, KY. We would ride them to the movies in Neon, KY. We would see movies like Roy Rogers and all the rest of the big guys, buy a Clark candy bar or popcorn.

Trains were wonderful to ride. You could sit and watch time pass by, trees, houses, people, smoke from the big engines.

We could ride most anywhere for a dime. The only thing, we didn't have too many places to go. Neon was it. This was our world as far as the train was concerned.

I would go to sleep at night with the train going by my house. The noise and the big light shinning in my window—my bedroom. My world.

Chapter Forty-Five
Rocks

Rocks were a big thing with us guys also. We threw rocks at everything—cars, trucks, each other. If we were not throwing rocks, we were throwing baseballs or basketballs.

The bathhouse was a big building as I said before. Often, I took a bath with my daddy. I will get back to the bathhouse in a minute.

As I said, rocks were a big part of our lives. One day, the train was coming through Seco. We were throwing rocks at the train. One of us boys threw a rock and hit a man in the caboose. Didn't mean to do it. Shit happens.

Some time later, a man came to school. He said he was a railroad detective. Who was this man?! He said someone was guilty of killing a conductor or a person who worked for the railroad, apparently from a rock thrown through a window of the caboose. If they found out who did this, they would be sent to Greendale in Lexington, KY—a prison for young boys. We all knew that was a bad place to be. None of us said anything about this. Still don't know what happened to this man. We probably don't know if we did it or not. Don't think we did.

To this day, we still don't know. Maybe the train detective was just trying to scare all the boys from all over not to throw rocks at the trains when they come by. Never did. I guess they got their message across.

About rocks, one day us guys were in the bathhouse taking a shower—we could do this. The older boys thought they were tough. One of them tied my pant legs together. That was not good. I put my shorts on, ran down the road and got a big red cinder (a piece of coal that had been used for heat). I picked it up and threw it. Won't reveal his name. I hit him in the head. He fell, big cut. I could hit a bird sometimes flying. Still pretty good. Dr. Wright put stitches in his head. He didn't tie any more pants.

What a part of growing up in the little town of Seco, KY. Sorry I hit him in the head, not really.

Chapter Forty-Six
Bathhouse—Basketball Court Indoor Dome

South East Coal Company moved out of Seco to Goose Creek above Neon, KY. Us boys got the best deal. We got the Bath House. The company built us a gym in the Bath House. We had light, concrete floor and goals on each end of the floor. We could have probably been the Harlem Globetrotters. We would play all day long, then take a warm shower, not warm, but as hot as we would like. And as long also. There was plenty of hot water from the coal that produced hot water.

Our own gym with a roof over it. We didn't know this at the time, but we were probably one of the first domes in the country. Can you believe this? In a little town of Seco, KY.

Chapter Forty-Seven
Dr. Wright—
His House and Pool

Dr. Wright was a most wonderful man. Everyone said he drank a lot. Who cared, he saved a lot of lives. Probably mine. I got sick with bronchial pneumonia every winter. He would come to my house and pull the stuff from my throat. I know he saved me many times. Thanks, Doc. I know you were a Christian man, probably more than the people that went to the little Methodist Church in Seco. I know you are in Heaven.

Dr. Wright lived in a big house in Whitaker. It was a big house. I was inside several times. They had a family. I think his wife was half crazy. Nobody ever saw her. They had more than any of us boys had ever seen—big house, swimming pool, big cars. But not the love and the main things a little boy needed to make his life great. No worrying, a nice bed and a mommie and daddy like mine. All boys have the greatest mom an dad, but this mommie is the big one.

All the kids got invited to a party at Dr. Wrights' house for some reason. Probably a birthday, who cared. We went. The pool was big but the water was so cold. Must have come out of the spring upon the hill.

The water came out of a big frog's mouth. Not a real frog. The frog was covered with moss from all the moisture. We tried to swim in the pool—too cold! We enjoyed all the stuff they had. Us guys left and went back to the wonderful world of our own....cowboys, Indians, baseball players, bike riders. A wild bunch of guys.

Thank you, Dr. Wright, for all these memories. You kept the boys of Seco well.

Chapter Forty-Eight
Poison Ivy

I got poison ivy every year. Hurt like hell. And itched very bad. I would get it so bad that Dr. Wright would give me heat lamp treatments to try to dry it up. I would lie on my belly, seemed I got most of it on my backside where I slid down the rocks and stuff. Got it on my feet—on top and bottom. One day, I woke up with big poison ivy blisters on the bottom of my feet. Could hardly walk. Of course, I went to Dr. Wright.

Dr. Wright was kind of a cool guy. Probably had some moonshine with a little cherry juice and cherries—they call it Cherry Pie. Pretty good stuff. I think I'll have another sip while writing this chapter.

Getting back to my feet. Dr. Wright came in, said hello and looked at my foot. Big blister on my foot. He brought a big tray with knives, scissors. Silver in color. He took what looked like a knife, put purple medicine on my foot, some kind of germ killer, I guess. I laid there. He took this knife and punched a hole in the big blister. Something squirted out of the hole. I thought it was a deadly poison. Enough to kill us boys. The gang of Seco, KY would no longer exist. Dr. Wright probably would have used it. We caused him enough trouble a few years of our young lives in Seco.

He then took a pair of scissors and cut the skin that was holding all the liquid. There was enough skin to cover a baseball.

Not really but to me it looked like it. He proceeded to put more purple stuff on what was left.

Again, it burned like hell. He told me to try to keep it clean for awhile. No wrapping or nothing. That was like telling me to jump over the moon. At least I walked out of the operating room on two feet. Felt really good. I was ready to get back into as much trouble as possible, whatever was left of the day. Thank you, Dr. Wright, for all the many things you did for us boys.

Don't know exactly how to start this. It seems all a sudden a lot of boys were having trouble with their tonsils. Don't know, don't care. All I knew, I didn't want to go to Dr. Wright unless I was dying. I sure didn't want him to put the scissors in my mouth.

Omar Champion was the first to have his tonsils removed. Best I can remember, Paul Patrick was next. I knew something wasn't right. And I knew I was not going. Maybe they were trying to get rid of us boys in Seco.

My big brother, Johnny, apparently was having some sort of trouble, sore throat, ears. I don't know. I guess Mom was afraid he would die. He was the next victim of the big tonsil removal in the hospital. Didn't sound too good to me. I remember the morning Mom took him to the big event of the day. I had to go with my mommie. We watched as they, the nurse, took my big brother away, never knowing if I would ever see him alive again. Suddenly, Johnny came running out of the operating room. Don't know what happened. He probably had a day in Hell. My mom, Johnny and myself went home. I think he ran home with the hospital gown on. Mommie said they only removed one tonsil. Don't know to this day, all I know is I still have my tonsils. I wasn't going to that room again. Don't know if Johnny went back to remove the other tonsil. I think he did. Took some nerve. They probably should have made a series or something about the hospital. Today, they would have: Abuse to children. None of us died, but sometimes, it was pretty close.

Us boys did whatever we needed to do to have fun—most of it was dangerous. One day, we decided to swing on grapvine. I really think this was some kind of ivy vine, but it worked. We had a favorite one way back in the hills. This thing would go out over a mine cave-in. Probably a 100 ft. down, once you started to swing out into midair. Probably the first parasailing.

One ride was my brother swinging out, when he came toward the beginning, can't remember who it was when Johnny came back. But he jumped on the rope vine and grabbed above Johnny's hands. They went out over the big deep cavern. Johnny couldn't hold both of them with his hands. He fell!! We all thought he was killed for sure. He rolled a pretty good ways down the big mine break. We slid down into the big ditch to get to him. I mean slid. Pretty good. Fun. Scary. Thank God, he was alive. My mom and dad would have killed me also if he had died. He took care of me when we were out like this.

We got him up, his arm was sorta out of being straight. We didn't know. We had a long way to walk to the hospital. We made it—all of us guys. The head nurse came and got Johnny. We followed him to the operating room. I swore I would never go there again. Dr. Wright came in. Johnny was lying down on this big white table. Everything was white or silver-looking in the room. Dr. Wright looked at his arm. Broke, of course. Don't know if Dr. Wright was drinking then or not. Anybody could tell it was broken. Dr. Wright mixed the white stuff with water, like plaster. He took bandage, wrapped it around his arm, then put this plaster over it. Doctor knew what he was doing. Looked like a masterpiece to me. He left. Everyone of us still living. What a day in Heaven. We probably went to the Seco Fountain to get a big milkshake. The Fountain was right below or downstairs.

For those that don't know, the Fountain is a restaurant something like I.H.O.P. but a lot nicer. Know what I mean.

A Little Boy in Paradise, Seco, KY

I was no more than 7-8. My daddy got sick one night. He was hurting pretty bad. I thought it as a bellyache or something. They couldn't find Dr. Wright anywhere. Finally, they found him. He came to the house. Checked Dad and sent him to the hospital. He had appendix trouble. Everyone said Dr. Wright was probably drinking when he came to our house. Who cares. People talk. Dr. Wright removed my daddy's appendix. Probably saved-his life. I know he did with the hands of God helping. I think I will have a little sip of my Cherry Pie Shine. Thanks, Doc.

Chapter Forty-Nine
Baseball at the Ballpark

South East Coal Company had their own baseball team, as did many other coal companies. We had the most beautiful baseball field, smooth as glass, soft dirt, perfect to catch a ground ball. The company had a few bleacher seats. Big screened back stop to catch the foul balls. We played every day during baseball season. We were all major league players. We didn't have too much equipment: a few baseballs, few bats. No chest protectors, no shin guards, no cups, no face masks. We made our own chest protector—wood bark from a tree, shin guards were the same. Worked. Used tape to get this to stay on your body.

We had enough guys every day to have ball games. We were the best, had no team names. No uniforms—shorts, tee shirts, tennis shoes—high tops, of course. No socks. We had Wilson baseball gloves. Rawlings baseballs, Louisville Slugger bats. They were the best. Didn't know at the time. Probably still the best. No metal bats—just wood. Sounds better, is better. Believe it or not, we bought our own stuff. Us guys sold corn, wood for fires, cut grass or whatever to buy stuff like sport's equipment. We would go home for lunch and then come back to play more baseball.

One day, as we were playing, these guys showed up to play a game of baseball. They said they came to play the Seco team, which was my Daddy's team. They were working in the mines. We were pretty good. We told them we would play them. They were from Perry or Knott County. They looked pretty good in practice. The best on our team chose who would play. we all had played during the game. I played third base, same as my dad. I think he was with me all the time. Dad was good, real good. Believe me or not, we won the ballgame. A bunch of boys from Seco, KY. They were men, but we were boys on a mission. They left the ball diamond and went home. We were home.

The team Dad played on was nothing but champions. They would work in the mine all day, take a bath in the bathhouse, then play a ballgame. These men were tough. Real tough.

My daddy played third base. He never missed a ground ball. He could throw a ball like a bullet and hit just as well. His biggest trick was to be on third base. If he thought the base runner was going to steal, the pitcher would throw the ball to Dad. Dad would fake throwing to the pitcher. The runner would step off the base and Dad would have the baseball in his glove. He would reach over and tag the runner out. Then, the fight would begin. They loved to fight. Not long, just fun, I guess.

Hate to interrupt this, but just got a phone call from my daughter, Rebecca. My grandson, Cal Welch (he has my middle name, was born on my birthday) as I am writing this about baseball, has made the high school baseball team at Tates Creek High School in Lexington, KY. You have to be very good to do this. My daddy, me, granddaddy, now my grandchild. Cal is a great player. I know he will do good. Great.

Getting back to Seco, KY. Roy Hill was a big man, tallest man I ever saw. He played first base, left handed. He would get up to bat, outfield was forever away. The company store was forever. Houses, creek must have been 2 or 3 football fields away. Roy hit a baseball one day. It went over the house, rolled and when it stopped, the ball was at the store when they got to it.

These guys could hit a ball 200 yards all day long. They all could have gone to Major League teams. My mom told me my dad could have gone. He tried out and made the team. I think she said Cleveland Browns. But he came home and married her. I guess he got a home run with her, they got me.

They worked hard and played hard. Drank hard whenever they could. My daddy always had a big grin on his face, just like Cal does now. I would go with Dad to different places to play ball. One night, we went to Pound, VA. to play. Mom didn't want me to go. Daddy said, "Don't worry." What a big joke that was.

I sat and watched the ballgame. We won, of course. Started home. I think the men might have a drink or two. We stopped to eat. Started home. I got sick on the food I ate and threw up 2 or 3 times. Probably too late for a little boy, I guess. Daddy told me not to say anything to Mom. I didn't. Good game and good food. We got home. What a day and night to remember. My daddy was a wonderful man, wish I could have him longer. I miss him. Mom asked me about the game and all. I told her it was great, the food too. Never did and never will tell her about this great day and night in my life. I went to bed and watched the light over our little church and railroad tracks, waiting for the train pulling the coal from the mines where the daddies worked. The big light on the front of the big engine. I went to sleep.

Chapter Fifty
The French Legion Army on a Desert

We decided to go to the movie to see something about men fighting in the desert. This was a Saturday when the movies were a dime. Serials and all. News from all over the world, cartoons and all. We got a Mounds bar of candy or popcorn of some kind. The movie started all in black and white. These men riding across the desert on horses. Seems like they should have had camels. We all agreed. Probably didn't have that many camels for the movie. They wore brown uniforms with brown caps and something in the back of their caps. I now know, it was to keep the sun out. They came upon the fort that they were going to protect. When they got there, it was under fire from the enemy. Whoever that was. Didn't know, didn't care. We didn't know what that was. We had no enemies. They fought all over the place. Sword fighting was the big thing. Swords flying everywhere. Also a lot of shooting. Men falling everywhere. They were on the roof of the fort. The French Foreign was winning. They killed many men. Don't know why people kill each other. Still don't to this day. They had swords and rifles. Everywhere men dying, swords sticking through the whole bodies and coming out the back.

When all this fighting was over, the French army won. What we didn't know, there was a man that was one of the captain's son.

Some big man. The wife or mistress that he wanted to save. They all met in the big middle yard of the fort. The French army won. The Captain of the French army got his girl or mistress or wife. Who knows. Still don't.

Us guys went out of the movie ready to fight the world. We were the French Foreign Legion of Seco, KY. We got to our paradise.

We tried to figure out how to dress like the French Foreign Legion soldiers. Didn't have much luck. But we did dress the best we could.

One day, we made swords out of plaster board. They were about an inch in width. Were made probably 3 ft. long. Put a little short piece to go across the long piece. Looked like a cross.

We needed someplace to fight. A high place to look like high sand dunes or something. We decided to go to the box cars. They were tall, long, looked like a good place to fight.

We got all dressed up like the French army to fight the enemy, but we fought each other. Some dressed normal; we killed each other and actually fell like dead. I was fighting like hell to not get killed, forgot the length of the box car (can't remember who I was fighting).

We got to the end of the box car. I know I had to get off or be killed by the enemy. There were steps on both ends of the box cars, but one end had only two steps for men to stop the cars. They would turn a big wheel to stop the car. I made the <u>big mistake</u>. I was going to escape from the enemy. I took two steps. Too bad. I fell on my back. Lucky I didn't hit on the rail track. Still was knocked out. Fell probably 15 feet. My buddy came to my rescue.

Again, they ran and got Dr. Wright. He came to make sure I wasn't dead. Probably wished I was. We caused him a lot of problems. But he was our doctor. I was not dead. Got going again after a while. Don't know who won the big fight, but we all went to town, our homes. We had fought a good battle in the desert. I was pretty sore from the fall, nothing serious.

We had spent a hard day, doing what we do. Covering the world. Very small to us.

I think my mom cooked supper. Probably chicken, potatoes, biscuits, even beans. I can't remember many meals at home, but I'm sure I had good food. This was called supper time then. Now, it is called dinner. Today, people don't have a time to eat. Just whenever they get hungry. Ain't that a bitch!

Most evenings our dads would meet on the Fountain Front—benches, steps. Us boys would play around, running, whatever.

Dad and the men were sitting and talking on the steps, laughing. Don't know what they were talking about. Baseball, women, liquor. Pretty good amen. I went over to Daddy, asked him if we could get an ice cream cone. He told me—in a minute. I turned around and my words were—"Well, shit." That was the wrong thing to say. <u>Big mistake</u>.

Daddy got up, got me, sat my ass down. He said we will get ice cream. I sat there until Daddy was done. He came and got me. We went into the Fountain and got my ice cream cone. Vanilla. Favorite still. We went outside, sat down on the steps and had our ice cream. He had one too. What a dad.

He didn't talk a lot. He probably asked me what I was going to do tomorrow. I probably told him us guys were going to the woods, who knows. We had our ice cream. We got up and walked home holding hands. I can still feel his hand holding mine. We got home ready to move for a good night's sleep.

Don't know what we did between now and bedtime. Mom would get me ready for bed. Bath, pajamas. Probably Roy Rogers, Gene Autry P.J.'s, maybe popcorn, cookies, milk. We had no TV to watch. Mommy would always put me in bed and kiss me goodnight. Still does when I go home. That was until she went into the nursing home. I will always be her little boy. That is fine with me.

Finally, I would get in bed. Pull the covers up. Look at all my pictures, wallpaper, all western stuff. Pictures of Roy Rogers, Gene Autry and Dale Evans, Whip Wilson, Hopalong Cassidy. Too many to mention. Getting ready for another day in paradise. Every day was a day of adventure.

I pulled the covers up, said a prayer, closed my eyes—gone. I knew my dad and mom were close to me, protected by them. Never worried that anyone would harm me. Pretty good feeling. What a place to live, a little town in a big valley of Seco, KY.

Chapter Fifty-One
Snakes—Fire Crackers

We, us guys, the Gang, were always in the woods. One day we caught a big, I <u>mean</u> Big black snake. Probably five, six feet long, maybe longer. Sometimes they would find a rabbit or something to eat. Swallow it whole. The big snake had a hump in its belly. We knew it had swallowed something. We laid the big snake down. Started behind the hump, kept pushing. Finally, a little rabbit came out of the snake's mouth. Dead, of course. The snake was not dead, still moving. We took the snake to town, not a good thing to do. This thing was big. We got to the store porch and someone said to take it to the Engineering Dept. They could measure it.

I was the one to do this.

I carried this big snake in the office. The snake was very limp, nearly dead, I guess. I went in. Mr. Champion, I believe, was there working. I laid the snake on the table. Mr. Champion looked up and went wild. I didn't know he was afraid of snakes. I ran out and left the snake with him. When I walked out, they were all laughing. They knew he was afraid. I didn't. I later told him I was sorry. He understood.

Still don't know how long the snake was. I can still see it on e big table on the white paper, moving slowly toward Mr. npion.

Mr. Champion was a very wonderful man. Very kind to all us boys. If only the people of this world could be as kind and gentle. Most of this family is gone now. I miss all of these folks.

Wouldn't it be good if one could live in paradise forever. Never getting old. Staying the same age which you loved best— little boys, little girls. But life goes on.

Thank you, Mr. Champion, for good memories and thanks for being in Seco, KY. A wonderful place to grow up in.

I know you are in Heaven now with the people of Seco, KY, that you know, from our little church. What a beautiful little church.

Firecrackers

The gang always had firecrackers, not only on the 4th of July. We were a smart bunch of guys. We did firecrackers all year long. They were very small, sometimes, they wouldn't even go off or make a noise.

Cherry bombs were the big ones. Very dangerous. We never got any of these. One day, don't remember who did this, but someone put a cherry bomb under a can, lit the fuse; it went off, blew the can and put the eye out of the boy who was holding the can. Us guys never did this kind of stuff.

Don't know what we had been doing all day. Probably been to the hills, playing ball, riding bikes.

We were on the store porch one evening. Doing nothing but sitting on the steps, chewing. A little bit of Beachnut tobacco. Seeing who could spit down the steps farther. Hard to do. We bummed a chew from the men.

We had a few firecrackers we had been shooting. One or two left. Mr. Preston was coming toward us. I think Omar Champion said, "Let's scare him." I was handed a firecracker; someone lit it. Mr. Preston stepped down on the sidewalk; I threw the firecracker. It went right on top of his hat. Went off!! The paper went everywhere. He turned around and said he was deaf, couldn't hear nothing. We all knew we were in trouble. We sat down on the steps. Mr. Preston left. We all continued to play or whatever.

It was getting time to go home for the day. I got home after a day of adventure; playing, fighting, probably smoked a little cornsilk, wrapped in a piece of brown paper bag. Strong but good. A little buzz. I was swinging on the porch and Daddy came out and sat down beside me. He asked me if I had thrown a firecracker at Mr. Preston. I said I didn't know he was coming down the steps.

Mr. Preston knew I threw the firecracker. I told him I did. He wasn't deaf after all. Daddy believed me. I never did tell him a lie. He said okay. Took my little hand, we were in a place of our own—in paradise of Seco, KY. Swinging, looking at the mountains. I had the most wonderful daddy ever. He always believed me. I miss him. Wish he could have been here with me to grow old. He would have been 100 years old now. My mom is 100 years old now. That's life. Don't know when we are going, but we all will.

As the preacher said one Sunday morning to his congregation—"Stand up if you are ready to go to Heaven." People stood up. One old man held up his hand. The preacher asked him what was it he wanted to say. The old man said, "I'm ready to go to Heaven, but I don't want to go right now." That's me. I ain't done raising cane (didn't want to say Hell).

Thanks for firecrackers, they were part of our life. Sorry, Mr. Preston. You were a very nice person. Very good man, father, sband. I had a lot of respect for you. Nice Suits, ties, pretty cool

Thanks Seco, KY. My little Heaven. We ate supper after Daddy and me left the swing. I went upstairs to my bedroom, took a bath and put on my Roy Rogers PJ's to go to bed. Waiting for the train to put me to sleep. No worries, waiting for another day of adventure. I closed my eyes. Gone.

Chapter Fifty-Two

Freewill Baptist Church

There are a lot of churches—Baptist, Methodist, Catholic, Pentecostal, Holiness. They all think if you don't belong to theirs, you will probably go to Hell. Is this not funny.

I went to the Methodist Church in Seco, KY. Very quiet. Not too much Amen stuff. Mr. Tuggle was the most wonderful pastor of all. Very quiet, good preacher. He would tell you about God in a good way. He would tell you that God loved you. That was enough for me and I loved him!

Snake handing was my favorite. This one church believed you could not die if you were bitten by a poisonous snake. I believe, but not this much. If this poisonous snake bites me, I will probably die. I want to go to Heaven, not right now. Know what I mean?

Mr. Pat Boggs of Jenkins, KY was the only man I knew that went to these events. He said he would take rattlesnakes and copperheads. Very deadly. He told me of one man who got bit by a rattlesnake. The man fell on the floor. Laid there and died. This was in Virginia, across Jenkins Mountain. I hope the man went to Heaven. He must not have believed enough.

My favorte church of all was the Freewill Baptist Church of Seco, KY. Maybe in Whitaker, very close to Seco.

My daddy loved this church. I would go with him. I don't k Mommy liked it much. She was more Methodist. Quiet. Like nily. Actually, pretty boring. The preacher would jump, holler real loud. Mr. Pike was his name. He sure could preach. They would talk in tongues, shake and shout. Us boys would go just to watch the women jump and shout. The more they shouted and swung their arms, the louder Mr. Pike would preach. They would roll in the floor and everything.

One night, one of the women knocked the warm morning stove over. Smoke went everywhere. They got it all cleaned up and went back to preaching and hollering as if nothing ever happened.

One week, there was a revival. Every night was a big deal. Lots of different preaching. They preached a long time. Lots of shouting, shaking, speaking in tongues. Sounded pretty good. Us guys (the gang) could do this. We did this when we did preaching by ourselves. I can still do it. Maybe I should have been a preacher.

One night, it really got wild; jumping, shaking. This one woman, can't reveal her name, she lived in Seco. She was shouting, waving her arms in the air. All of a sudden her big boobs, or breasts, fell, or came out, of the top. I guess she held her arms too high. They were bouncing. when she realized, she quickly took care of the matter. It didn't seem to make too much concern for the revival.

Maybe some men didn't get saved that night, but they sure did get to see some big boobs.

The Gang went to our homes.

I went to my secret hideaway with the Lone Ranger, Roy Rogers, my home in Seco, KY. My bedroom looking at the train coming past my bedroom, church, with the big light shining. Going to sleep. No worries. My mommy and daddy close by. I knew I would awake for another day in paradise.

Chapter Fifty-Three
Vacations—Smokies—Tennessee

My daddy thought the only place to go on vacation was the Smokies in Tennessee. He loved this place. I guess he planned all year for this trip, like I did with our girls—wherever we went.

Mommy would pack a big basket of food—I mean a lot. Crackers, ham salad, cookies, popcorn, Kool-Aid, Vienna sausage, potted meat, cheese (Velveeta, of course). Seems like we ate the whole time. I didn't mention egg sandwiches for early morning breakfast. We would drive and stop at a roadside area. Not like today. No big rest stops. I mean pretty primitive area, on the ground. We would eat and then travel more.

My mom talked the whole time we were on the road. Dad listened to her and so did I.

Daddy loved to stop at all the fruit markets on the way. Must have been hundreds. Every one of them, he would stop. He loved apple cider. He would get a big cup of apple cider. Loved this stuff. I could drink a little. He would buy a peach, apple, or whatever they had. We would get back in the car. Drive more until the next apple cider stop. I would sleep, wake up, eat more. It took all day to get to the Smokies, no big roads like today.

Mommy was always worried we would get lost, get eaten by bears or something. She drove Daddy crazy. We would stop, get gas at some pretty isolated place. Mommy would swear we were lost. We would go in some toilet and pee. We would get back in and drive some more.

Daddy would drive, Mommy would tell Daddy we were lost. Daddy would finally tell Mommy to shut up, be quiet. You have talked all day. Of course, that didn't sit too good with her. But this is what she did; talk, talk. She has done this all my life, still does. At 101 years old, still does love to talk. What a wonderful person, mother, Christian. If she doesn't go to Heaven, nobody will. She is a saint.

We would finally get to the Great Smoky Mountains. What a place. We always stayed at the Black Bear Motel. I don't know if it was in Pigeon Forge then. I guess it was. We would stop, go to the motel room after Daddy would pay for the room. It was called the Black Bear Motel because they had a big black bear in a cage. The bear was big. At the motel entrance, you had to see it first. Mom was scared to nearly dying. She was terrified. She was afraid of most anything. We would finally go to bed. Mom probably didn't sleep much. Afraid the bear would get out of the cage it was in.

In the morning, we would get up, go out for breakfast. I would eat this stuff.

Dad would tell us to get ready. We were off for a wonderful vacation adventure. He loved the Smokies. We would get in the car and Mom guarded me like a warrior, afraid the bear would come out of the cage.

We would drive through Gatlinburg, the main town in the Smokies. Wasn't much there then, very narrow street, very few stores. Cherokee Indians everywhere. We would drive through town. Going to see the bears with my daddy. Looked forward to seeing them. it was a long ride across the mountain, traffic very slow, narrow road. Cars would stop to see the bears. They were many. Babies, mommies. I guess there were daddy bears too. Daddy had a camera to take pictures of the bears. Mom was hysterical, mad, scared we would be eaten by bears. We stopped at a pull off place; a big barrel was there for garbage. It was smoking. This big bear came over to get whatever was in it. Food, I guess. This man went over toward the bear. He wasn't sure what was going to happen to him. This big bear came after him. He ran like Hell. Barely got away. I hope he's still living. I'm sure he's a saved man now.

Mommy was screaming to Daddy to get away. Daddy had a camera. He took a picture of the man running from the bear from the barrel.

Dad loved this kind of stuff. Mom was a nervous wreck all the time. He would get in the water on the mountain stream; he loved it. We would see baby bears, mommy bears; there were plenty of bears then. Not now.

We would get back in the car and drive some more across the mountain. It was a slow drive to Cherokee, North Carolina.

We would drive into this town. He loved this. Indians everywhere—I mean real Cherokee Indians. We would park the car, get out and shop in all the stores. Mommy would not let me out of her sight. Afraid someone would kidnap me.

Daddy would always find apple cider everywhere. I think Mom thought there was alcohol in the stuff. We would watch the Indians dance to the drums. They were really good. All the feathers, headdresses, colors of the rainbow, moccasins. They were a pretty people. What the United States of America did to the Indians. I guess I would have fought for the Indians if I had been there.

We would shop the whole day, find a place to eat. I would always buy Indian stuff; a headdress, tomahawk, drum. I was a real Cherokee Indian.

After a hard day in Cherokee, we would head back to Gatlinburg. Daddy would stop at the first sight of people stopping to watch the bears. I would wade in the stream, very cold water. Felt good. Hot day, no air conditioning in the car.

We always had food to eat. Mom would get the basket. Had more food by the creek. What fun for a boy from Seco, KY.

We would finally start back again. It took a long time across the mountain to our motel room at the bear motel. Again, Mommy would worry about the bear getting out of the cage and eating me up. We would bathe and go to bed. Don't know where we all slept. I didn't care. I was getting ready for another day of adventure in the Smokies. Mom probably stayed up most of the night worrying that the bear might get me. I was ready for anything. I had my tomahawk and Indian headdress, drums and moccasins. I would wake up ready to fight the world.

I don't know where we ate breakfast, some place Dad found. Eggs, biscuits, gravy, pancakes. He loved to do this. So did I with my family. Linda, Deb, Beck. What a group. Right, girls?!!

We would walk the streets of Gatlinburg, shop more, go back to Bear Motel and swim in the little pool. The big bear was pretty. Black, shining.

I guess my most wonderful memory of the vacation was when we would go back to Gatlinburg the last night of vacation. My daddy and me were sitting on a bench in Gatlinburg at night—real Indians were walking toward us. Daddy took my hands and covered them. He said, "Look at the real Indians." He was part Cherokee himself. Me too. What a wonderful daddy I had. I miss him so much.

We would shop some more, get some candy at the Old Smokie Mountain Candy Company. It was good. So many things to see as a little boy. We sure did have a big time, me and my daddy. After shopping and a good day seeing Indians, food. I was a real Indian now. Still am.

I guess my mommy was ready to go to bed. Probably wore out.

We would get up early. My daddy wanted to see more stuff, have a big breakfast, walk in Gatlinburg (not very big then). Daddy and I would sit on the benches and actually talk to the Cherokee Indians. We would walk until Mom got ready to go, that was it. We went back to the motel to swim or whatever, watch the bear in the cage, go eat, get ready to go to bed.

I guess we stayed three or four days then headed back home. Mommy was ready. No bears, no Indians. She didn't like this stuff.

Daddy still stopped at all the apple cider stands on the way. Every fruit stand, peaches, apples. Whatever he saw he would stop. We would drive-stop, eat, drive more. Mom talked a lot. Still does. Got back home. Was a very long ride, but it was always fun.

We would get back home late. I would go to my favorite place: my bedroom. I would take all the stuff I got on vacation. All Indian stuff: headdress, tomahawk, peace pipe that really worked. We later actually smoked corn silk in it. I would get ready for bed, go to sleep, wake up for another day full of adventure. I was back home in Seco, KY. No worries. Got with my buddies and showed them the stuff I had from vacation.

Thanks to my Mommy and Daddy for a wonderful life they have given me. I will always remember the vacations in the Smokies. I still like the taste of apple cider. I think of my dad when I drink it. Still see his gold tooth after a drink. I miss him so much.

Chapter Fifty-Three
Funeral Service at Seco Methodist Church

This was not something to remember but I did.

On the day of the funeral (I won't tell the dead man's name) what a day this was. A very sad day. He got killed in the mine. Rock fall or something inside the mine. The little church was full of people. Singing all the old songs, Amazing Grace, Bringing in the Sheaves. All that stuff. Everybody was sitting in the pews crying. Finally, they would bring the casket through the doors from outside up through the aisle of the church. Archie Craft owned the Funeral Home in Whitesburg, KY. He was a very nice man, a good person and loved the people. This was his business. He did a good show.

They would put the casket in front. The thing about Archie Craft is that he had black hair, dressed nice, had a limp, very pale-looking sorta like a ghost. Didn't smile at all during the time he was doing his job. Archie would open the casket, fix everything, walk back down the aisle. Limping and all.

The story I heard from a little boy is that he got hurt in the mine. Broke his leg or something that was why he limped. His leg was actually crooked. This was when he got into the funeral home business. Fixing dead bodies to look good was a lot easier than working in the mines.

When the preacher finished preaching about how good and all, this dead person was going to Heaven no doubt. No matter what he did on earth. All good.

Archie Craft walked up through the aisle, limping, very somber. He would walk up to the casket, very gentle. Put the top down over the casket after everyone would come by and look at the body, or whoever was in the casket. He was very kind and gentle at what he did. He was in front. The men would carry the casket out, put it in the hearse and take him and bury him.

After the funeral, time for food, plenty of this stuff.

Everyone would go home, leaving the deceased family alone. Probably not knowing what to do without their loved one. This was the way it was in Seco, KY as a little boy. Very sad day, but what can I say. The last thing we could do was look at the dead body in the casket. Everyone in the little church would march by the casket. Sure did not look good to any of us guys, but we did.

We would leave the church, go home, change clothes, then begin to play, or whatever else.

This was a very long day for everyone. Night time would come; time for me to go to bed. Take a bath, put p.j.'s on and get in bed looking at Roy Rogers, Gene Autry, the train. Finally going to sleep. Waking up in Seco, KY, my Heaven. Getting ready for another day.

Chapter Fifty-Five
Vacation to Ohio

This was not the place to go but Daddy had a niece there. His sister's daughter, I think. My papa and mama raised her. Daddy stole her from her mother and brought her home to them on a train from Whick, KY.

Martha Lou grew up and moved to Ohio. She was a wonderful person, very big, but beautiful. Always laughing and having a wonderful time.

The story is her mother moved to New Orleans and opened a whore house. That is what she was, apparently. Became very wealthy. She died there and was buried in one of the crematoriums. With all the honors of jazz bands and all. Pretty good way to go.

Daddy would visit Martha Lou and her husband Carl. A very weird man. I think he was actually crazy. He would wash his bread and forks and stuff before he ate. Nothing to do except walk in the backyard. We stayed around, walked, sat in chairs. Daddy had a good time.

We did go to Cincinnati ball game. Carl got the tickets from someone he knew. He did not eat anything. Daddy and I got a hot dog, pop, and I think Daddy got a beer. He probably needed one. Carl was crazy. I guess Martha Lou found a man like her. Someone who would take care of her.

We would stay a few days with them. Daddy loved Martha Lou. Then we would head back home. I'm sure Mommy was glad to get on the road. She didn't think much of Carl, weird man. Sorta mentally ill—personality, dress and all. As I said, he washed his bread, forks, spoons. Whatever he used. Martha Lou would fix breakfast. Real good stuff, eggs, bacon, brown gravy. She was a country girl. Don't know much more of what we had. This is my favorite meal. I loved eggs. Still do.

It wasn't a long ride back home. Daddy didn't stop too many times like he did going to the Smokies, no apple cider and all that stuff. Don't remember much about stopping, probably did to eat a little and pee.

Again, I got back to my little bit of Heaven or all of it in my little bed in Seco, KY. Thanks to my mommy and daddy for another day in paradise.

Chapter Fifty-Six

Virginia Woman— Dry Cleaners

What a life in Seco, KY as a boy.

We had dry cleaners from Neon, Whitesburg and Virginia. The one from Virginia was called Norton Dry Cleaners.

One day, I was at the Fountain where Mom worked. The dry cleaning truck pulled up outside. This woman got out and came into the Fountain. She lived in Seco. I was sitting there on a stool. She looked at me. Didn't know then just how pretty she was. She asked my mom if it would be okay if I rode with her to deliver the dry cleaning. Mom said yes. Sounded good to me. Didn't get out of Seco too much, especially with a pretty woman. She wore plain clothes, more tight than normal. She had pretty feet, nails polished. She knew how to drive the truck.

It was hot this day, very hot. When we got in the van, I didn't have a place to sit. She said sit on the step, so I did. It was hot, the door was open on the van, hot breeze. Better than nothing. She would stop and deliver the cleaning at the houses. I would sit and wait for her. She climbed in and out. Hot as it could be. She had water to drink and asked if I would like some. We were in Jenkins at this time. We were sitting there hot as hell. I drank the water she had handed me. She then took my hand and pulled me to her lap. I didn't know what to do, too young, I guess. She touched me all over. I was scared. She knew it and let me go.

What a day in the dry cleaning business. She sure was pretty. Looked like a movie star.

Days are gone, so are the memories. I am sure you are in Heaven. You sure could drive good.

Another day in Seco, KY. Going to bed now, to my room of peace and harmony. Watching the train go by waiting for tomorrow.

Chapter Fifty-Seven
Bike Rides to Pine Mountain

What a trip this was. All day. We would plan it with care. Starting with food, same stuff—potted meat, Vienna sausage, wieners, crackers, bananas that Mr. Combs would give us at the store. Also apples, water, of course. There was a big spring on Pine Mountain. You could stop and get a drink of the wonderful stuff. They stopped this later, said it was no good. Didn't kill anyone. I knew then the world was going to Hell.

We would gather at Seco Company Store early. It was a long trip. All day, but the gang could handle it with no problem. We were the toughest.

We would leave the store, ride across the railroad tracks, past a few houses. Go past our little Methodist church, across the bridge of Kentucky River. This is where it begins. Up the hill out of Seco, KY. I love it.

We would start pedaling our bikes. Maybe 10-12 of us. We would pass each other, that is how it is when moving at a good pace.

We would ride to Milestone Company Store. Stop, go in and get a pop, grapette, or Pepsi. We would charge it to our daddy on his account at Seco. Same company. I didn't know at the time how hard my daddy worked for me. I miss him and his smile. I could do anything.

We would take off again on this long journey to Pine Mountain. We would ride along the river, cool all the time, up and down the hills. Ride past cemeteries where all our relatives were buried. We would stop and get a drink of water. There was one place we would stop. They sold everything. Rabbits' feet, they said it would bring you good luck if you carried one. Didn't seem to be very lucky for the rabbit. Pretty cool place. There was a cemetery across the road. We all said they should have bought a rabbit's foot. Too late.

We would finally get to the place, Pine Mountain Junction. Left—went to Cumberland, KY across the mountain. Straight— went to Whitesburg, KY. Not much more to say.

We stopped to rest awhile. We had traveled maybe five- seven miles. Very tough. A long ride ahead, but we were the gang and nothing could stop us.

We started the long ride up the mountain. We had kinfolk all the way. But I had one at the foot of the mountain. Hossie Webb was his name. I didn't know at the time how much he meant to me later in years.

We began up the road, riding some and walking some. Long ride and walk. Stop a lot and look out over the beautiful mountains, down in the valleys at all the little homes below. All the people living in their own little world. Not caring about nothing. Too bad. Know what I mean. We would see airplanes flying high above us. Looked pretty to us little boys. We finally got to the top of Pine Mountain.

The park ranger station was at the top. We would walk to the tower and look up. We could not go to the top and look out over the mountains, probably a very pretty sight to see. We would sit a bit, take a drink of water. Eat a little bit of our food, had plenty of stuff to eat.

We would finally be ready to start down Pine Mountain. We would try to go as far as we could go without using our brakes first. This was a very long trip. We would fly, too fast to describe! I mean flying around the curves. I don't remember who was first or last, we didn't care. What a trip down Pine Mountain. You should go there some day.

We would get to the bottom and eat some Vienna, wieners or bananas that Mr. Combs had given us at the Seco Store, crackers and water. The owners didn't like for him to do this, but he did. Thanks, Mr. Combs, for this. I know you are in Heaven with all the people in Seco, KY. Not many left.

We began the long trip back home. This was an all day trip for us. We would stop at the Milestone Store, which was part of South East Coal Company also. We would go in and get a pop, banana or whatever we wanted. Charged it to Daddy's account. What a way to live, not knowing what our Daddies did to give us this life.

We would then start again, not too many more miles, maybe 6 or 7. By the time we got back home, it was time to eat again, take a bath and go to bed. What a day. Mommy cooked supper, don't know what. The same stuff—meat, macaroni, greens, cheesecake.

I would get ready for bed. Tired and ready. Look at my heroes: Roy Rogers, Gene Autry, Whip Wilson, Lone Ranger and Tonto. My favorite Indian of all. Oh, tough man.

Looking at the railroad tracks. Big locomotives coming down the track. Every night. I mean every night. Same time. I can still hear the sound of the tracks clinking. Sounds good to my ears. I loved it then, love it now.

Going to sleep now. Another day tomorrow in Seco, KY. In Heaven. What a place to live. Thanks to all.

What a supper with my mommy and daddy. I miss them so much. I wish everyone could have had a life like mine.

Chapter Fifty-Eight
Carlie Fitch—
Store, Cigars—First One

Carlie Fitch lived next to us in Seco. His daddy was Mr. Fitch, who took me to the movies in Neon, KY, bought booze also there. At the Hub. He was quiet a few years older than me. I always looked at him very highly.

He was working at this little store in Whitaker, sorta like a 7 to 11 now. Think about it. You could buy a few things there. They also sold cigarettes, Prince Albert, Bull Durham pipe tobacco, pop and a few groceries.

Carlie smoked cigars. They always smelled good to me. The only thing I smoked was corn silk or rabbit tobacco. Neither one of them was too good.

One day, I was in the store, just happened to go see Carlie. He would always give me something. Maybe a grapette pop. I guess we talked a little bit. He was smoking his cigar. Smelled good. I asked him for a smoke. He said your mother would kill me if I gave you one. I told him not to worry. She would not know. So he gave me one. Lit this cigar up. Man, did it taste good. Thought I was in Heaven. Smelled good to me. I smoked a lot of it and then I began to get sorta sick or something. I told Carlie I was feeling sick. He said to me—"Smoke more." The more I smoked, the sicker I got, until I couldn't smoke anymore. I went out on the porch of the store and puked. Dizzy. Felt like shit. Mad at Carlie. I didn't know what to do or tell my mommy when I got home.

Carlie came out and said I needed to smoke more. He was laughing. Don't smoke these things. I got home sick. Mommy asked me why I was sick, and I told her Carlie made me smoke a cigar at the store where he was working. When he got in, she asked him about it. He said he did but Obie will probably not smoke anymore cigars. To this day, I smoke cigars and my pipes. Love cigars. At least 3 a week or more. Love my pipes. I have many I smoke.

I thank Carlie for his mistake. Thanks, Carlie. I love you.

I must tell this. I didn't see Carlie for years after we got older. He was living in another state, I think. But he was a big U.K. fan and so am I. He was in to football. I met him at a U.K. and Tennessee football game accidentally. Just walking around. After that day, we went to the U.K. games together. We would meet in the big parking lot at the stadium. Carlie liked his booze and so did I. He would wear a jacket that had places to put your shotgun shells in but he put those little airline bottles in them. Perfect. I would buy two half pints of vodka. I wore western boots. I put one bottle in one boot and one in the other. Of course, we had a few before the game started.

Carlie would take one of the little bottles out of his jacket. One drink. Gone. I mixed my vodka with a cup of ice. Pretty strong stuff. The first half went pretty well. U.K. didn't win too many games. By the time the game was over, Carlie and I were pretty well shot, but we managed to survive this night.

Thank you, Carlie, for these times with you. I can still see you giving me the wonderful cigar. I'm smoking one right now. Made in Cuba.

What a time in Seco, KY. You are still living at this writing. I hope you will live long enough to read this book about Seco, KY. Love you, my friend.

Chapter Fifty-Nine
Tennis Courts & Ping Pong

To this day, I don't know why they ever made tennis courts in Seco, KY. But they did. Very nice, black top with very high fence so the balls wouldn't go over. But the company, South East Coal people, the big wheels saw this somewhere. A big city, I guess.

This was great for us boys. Don't know where we got the tennis rackets, balls. Probably the company gave them to us. We all learned to play pretty good. All day. Loved this game. I figured they thought it would keep us busy and not cause trouble. Never did see adults playing But sure had a good time. No way they could bring

New York to Seco, KY. Very different places. The people in the cities were crazy. Had nothing to do. We sure did.

I don't know why they didn't build a big swimming pool. I guess they thought we had the creek to swim in.

We spent many days at the tennis courts until another season would come, Fall too cold to play tennis or whatever. Tired of tennis.

Some days in the summer it would rain real hard. Very hot. We would go to the tennis courts. Somewhere, we found water pistols. Took them to the tennis courts. We would fill them up with water on the court. Shoot each other with them. What a time we had. It didn't take much to make us happy. We would then go to the store, get something to eat. Same stuff. Maybe bologna, crackers, pop as usual and maybe a banana.

Another day in my little town of Seco, KY. My Heaven.

All of us guys would go to our homes to see our moms and daddies, eat a big supper, go outside and maybe swing on the front porch or get an ice cream at the Fountain.

Roger Rudd and Obie

Time would come to go to bed, take a bath and put my p.j.'s on. Mabye my Roy Rogers' p.j.'s or maybe Gene Autry. Cover up with my wonderful, warm covers, listen to the train. Going to sleep was easy. Getting ready for another day with buddies Roger Rudd, Ben Osborne, Clyde Quillen, Teddy Quillen, Omar Champion, Tony Taylor, Peanut Hall, Danny Hall. Maybe some I missed. Thanks, for all the memories. I love you all. Maybe some of you are still around. Maybe you will read this. There were many more boys, but this made up the gang.

Chapter Sixty
Ping Pong

We didn't know much about this game of ping pong. The company at Seco, KY put tables upstairs in the company store. Big room. They said we could play anytime we wanted to. Probably to keep us out of trouble. This game was a lot of fun. There were two tables, paddles and balls. It wasn't hard to learn to play. Since we all played baseball. Hit the ball. I was always fast with my hands and eyes. This was my game. I could put a twist on the ball, the buddies could not believe the action. I love the game of ping pong. We played a lot, all year long, especially in the winter. The big room was warm. All we had to do was go downstairs to the store and get some food. Maybe a slice of bologna, crackers and R.C. Cola. What a life. Us boys lived in paradise, but didn't know it. Our daddies worked all day for us to do this. Thanks, Dad. I miss you so much.

This is the way it was in Seco, KY. No worries. Loving, caring, giving. Loving God, living the Godly life, loving your neighbor, helping each other. Thank you, Seco, KY. Thank all of you parents. I know all of you are in Heaven. I know God took all of you there.

Thanks for the ping pong tables.

Chapter Sixty-One
Boy Scout

The Boy Scouts were a little part of my life. I joined the Scouts because all the boys did. Most of them were different from me. Not all. The gang did also. We had a good time, went many places, Dewey Lake to camp out for a weekend. Swim, eat lots of food, good time. Rode a big bus to these places, lots of fun.

I guess the Scouts decided to have a big jamboree at the cabin in Seco. The one us guys camped in at the time.

We sat around the big campfire. They fixed food on the fire, the Scout Masters. Didn't like them much. We ate some good food. After we ate, the men would put on a big show for us.

One night, we were sitting by the big fire and the Scout Master was telling a story about this big man that lived in the mountains. Big beard, pretty rough lookin (the talker). A lot about this. All of a sudden, the fire went up this big cable into the woods and this big bearded man slid down this cable into the fire and out. We were scared to death. we thought it was our death. The man was the Scout Master. Pretty cool. A good time. After eating, we went to our tents, slept good. Got up, they fixed a big breakfast. Us guys went home. That was the end of the Boy Scouts for me and the gang.

We went home to the little town of Seco, KY. Played some, I guess. Finally, it was time to go to bed. Getting in my little bed, my mommy would come in my bedroom, tuck me in my bed. She never did forget to say "I love you, Obie Welch". I would tell her, "I love you, Mommy." Then I would go to sleep. Waiting for another day in Heaven.

Chapter Sixty-Two
Omar Champion & My Pony

I am beginning to end this book.

Omar told me that Daddy was having some kind of argument with my mommy about my pony making too much noise. I had him tied to a post or line. Daddy came out of the house and hit my pony square in the head. My pony fell to the ground. This is what Omar told me that happened. This is true, I guess, from him.

Omar was a part of Seco, KY, still is. I sorta miss this place. I miss Kona, Millestone, Thornton. Still very pretty, but lost in the luxuries of the world.

Thanks, Omar, for this short chapter. I love you and thanks for telling me this. It sure was great in Seco, KY.

Going to bed now.

At Mom's funeral.

Chapter Sixty-Three
Zeek Jones—Big Bull Dog

Zeek lived in Seco with his mom and dad for awhile. Larry was his brother. Their daddy was Jim Jones, a very fine man.

Daddy and Jim went to Ohio to get a job. They didn't stay long. Came home. Didn't like the North. They moved to Millestone. The boys would come to Seco, KY. We went to school together.

The ballpark was the place to be. Some man, don't know who he was, would fly planes. Remote control. A big, big white bull dog would run after the planes. Zeek was afraid of this. He thought the dog belonged to me. Don't know what happened to the dog. Pretty.

Thanks, Zeek, for this wonderful memory. I love you. Miss you.

Another short story about Seco, KY.

He was at my mother's funeral.

Chapter Sixty-Four
Willard Rudd—
What a Man and Friend

This is a very short story. I will now begin the ending of this story, if I can. A book of memories I can never describe to you.

Willard and I talked a very long time, so close to the memories of Seco, KY. We could not get close enough. We had memories. I know I will not see him again. He kept coming to me to talk some more. I love you Willard Rudd. Can't say enough how good it was to see you.

I saw Omar, Zeek and Willard at my mother's funeral. They loved my mom very much.

Chapter Sixty-Five
The Ending of my Life in Seco, KY

This last chapter starts with the beginning when I was born. My mother, Eva, I love you—This is hard to write.

This book was dedicated to my mom, in the beginning until the end. And now it is the end.

Mom died on the 21st day of June, 2013. Her birthday was the 20th. Dad died on her birthday on the 20th. She was 101 years and one day. She had all this planned, I guess. She was tough, knew what she wanted. She was a beautiful woman. I guess this is why Daddy married her. He knew what he wanted and he got her. You did real good, Dad.

My mom kept me under her arms all her life. I knew this, still do. She protected me all the time. Even when I wasn't with her. When I was sick with pneumonia, my little head was hot with fever, she would take care of me.

I can still see her in the Fountain in Seco, KY behind the counter. Fixing me a big hamburger and fries. Real good. Beautiful person. She probably could have been in Playboy magazine. Believe me.

I can still see her fixing breakfast for me. Cream of Wheat, toast or biscuits. Making me eat it. Cod liver oil, of course, was the first thing I saw.

I can still see her getting me ready for church. Hair combed, ears clean, shirt in pants, shoes shined. She always told me to keep my shoes shined and my ears clean. That's what everyone looked at. To this day, I still do this.

She would tell me to go and sit on the steps or in the swing until church time. You know what I did? Exactly what she said.

I can still feel her hand holding mine while swinging on the porch in Seco. People walking by on the sidewalk in front of our house. No worries, no troubles. Didn't have T.V. I guess I thought everyone in the world was white like me. Don't know when I realized, not so. Enough on this.

We would listen to country music on our little radio. Elvis Presley was just beginning his career.

I can see Daddy teaching her how to drive. They would go to the ballpark. I would be in the back seat. What an event that was. She did get her license. Never quit driving until she was 95 years old or so.

Chapter Sixty-Six
Stack Cakes—Molasses, Apple Sauce and Shuck Beans— Bags of Cookies

I guess Mommy learned to make them from her mom or so she told me. She would roll little balls of flour, lard, cinnamon, bake them in a black skillet. Put apples between each layer. They were good.

Shuck beans were green beans dried in the sun. She would let them dry out until they were brown and very small. Less than a half the size. A handful would make a quart or more when cooked.

I knew someday she would quit making this. The last stack cake she gave me and the last shuck beans, I knew one thing. I would keep them until I died. I put them in our freezer. Still have them. I still look at this knowing my mommy's little hands made them for me. I still have two bags of little cookies. Don't know the name of them. We called them Snicker Doodle cookies. Good.

Thanks, Mom, for all you did for raising me to what I am. I know you were proud of me. I love you and sure do miss talking to you.

Chapter Sixty-Seven
My Mommy

Every child loves his, or her, parents equally. But girls maybe go to Daddy more in ways. But the boys, their mommy is the #1. No doubt.

There is something special between a boy and his mommy.

Here I am 72 years old writing this. Still thinking like a little boy. It has been three weeks since she went to Heaven. Sure would like to see her. I do, I guess.

She carried me for 9 months, I promised I would carry her last trip on her way to Heaven. I did. I kept my promise. Never thought it would ever happen. We can't live forever—But she did. What a life she lived.

I love you, Mom. Don't know how to handle such a loss. I know you are telling me it's okay. I'm with your daddy now. Everything is fine.

How does one quit writing about one's mother. Can't seem to find an end to this. Every day I want to talk to her. I guess it will get better. It has been a month. This book is for you.

This book is dedicated to my mother.

To all the little boys out there; no mater how old you are, 10 years old, 40 years old or 70 years old, remember your mother. She was the one that brought you into this world—you should be one to carry her to Heaven someday.

If you read this, I thank you so, so much.

Obie W. Spicer, Jr.

May God bless you.
Thanks.

Obie Welch Spicer, Jr.
Seco, KY
Main Street

CPSIA information can be obtained at www.ICGtesting.com
Printed in the USA
LVOW01s0338070815

449068LV00007B/12/P

9 781937 508395